FOLK·TALES·&·FABLES·OF
EUROPE

FOLK·TALES·&·FABLES·OF
EUROPE

Robert Ingpen & Barbara Hayes

DRAGON'S WORLD

Dragon's World Ltd
Limpsfield
Surrey RH8 0DY
Great Britain

© David Bateman Ltd & Dragon's World 1992

Text Editor Molly Perham
Editor Diana Briscoe
Art Director Dave Allen
Editorial Director Pippa Rubinstein

British Library Cataloguing in Publication Data
The catalogue record for this book is available from the
British Library.

ISBN 1 85028 169 6

Typeset in Bookman.
Printed in Italy

Contents

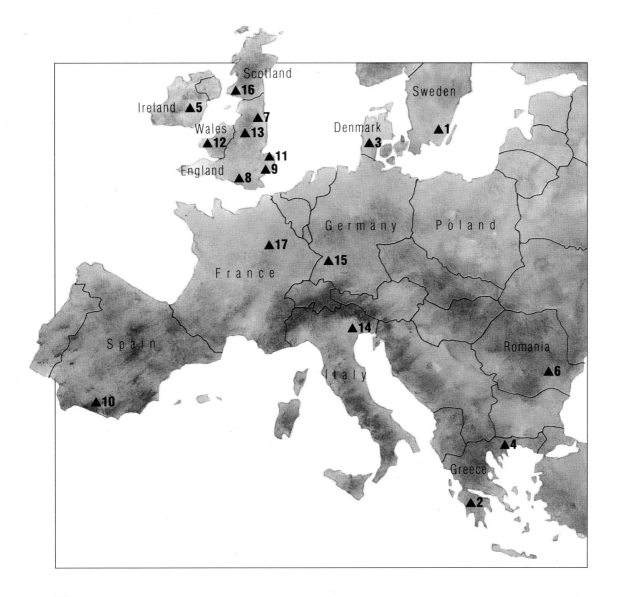

Europe

1

The Apples of Youth

The Vikings lived in Scandinavia, Denmark and northern Germany. They were warlike, seafaring people. During the eighth to the eleventh centuries they raided places across most of western and southern Europe, often settling in the lands they had conquered. It is thought that they sailed as far as North America in their longships. The Vikings told stories about their heroes and their gods. These are known as Norse legends.

When the glaciers retreated at the end of the last ice age, northern Europe was a dangerous and evil place. Only the gods were young and beautiful – they were the hope of the world.

Ugly dwarfs worked below the ground, where they collected gold, silver and jewels. They were clever smiths and forged beautiful goldwork and fine swords. But they spent their lives crawling about like maggots beneath the surface of the earth. They envied the youth and freedom of the gods. The first giants who lived at Jotunheim were jealous of the gods too. They were ready to attack at the slightest sign of weakness.

The gods were called Aesir. They saw chaos all around them and created Midgard, a garden in the middle of the earth. One day Odin, the father of the gods, with Hoenir, the bright god of the sun, and Loki, the arch-deceiver, the fascinating unreliable god of fire, were strolling through Midgard. There they saw two trees: the ash and the elm. From each tree they carved a log into a human form. Odin gave the logs souls. Hoenir gave them the power of movement and the gifts of hearing, seeing and feeling. Loki gave them blood and the fire of life. This was how the first man and woman were created; everyone is descended from them.

Then the Aesir decided to make a home for themselves. They crossed the wide River Ifing, whose waters never froze, to the broad plain Idawold, set high above Midgard. In the centre of this lovely and sacred place they built Asgard, the home of the gods.

There was to be neither quarrelling nor bloodshed in this beautiful city. There would be harmony as long as it was ruled by the gods. The Aesir also built the rainbow bridge, Bifrost, so that they could travel down to Midgard and return.

Iduna lived in Asgard. She was the wife of Bragi, the god of poetry, and she was the keeper of the golden apples of youth. The gods of Asgard did not stay young naturally; they could age, just as the mortals did. But they stayed young and strong by eating apples from Iduna's magic casket.

The frost giants and the dwarfs longed to eat the golden apples of youth as well, but Iduna never left Asgard and the apples stayed safe in their magic casket. When Iduna took an apple from the casket and gave it to a god, another apple would appear magically to take its place. The beautiful Aesir seemed secure in their eternal youth.

One day Odin, Hoenir and the tricky, unreliable Loki set out on a journey through Midgard as they often did. They walked for many hours, checking how the human beings they had created were getting on.

By the evening the gods were tired and hungry, so they killed an ox and built a fire to roast it. After resting for a while, Odin reached for some meat, expecting it to be cooked and sizzling with running fat. To his disgust it was still raw.

The gods stoked up the fire and put on some more wood. They waited a while until they were certain that the meat would be ready to eat. Once more Odin leaned forward over the blazing fire and tried to slice some tasty roast ox to put into his empty stomach. But the meat was still as raw as if it had never been near the fire.

The three gods realised now that some sort of magic must be at work. Looking around, they saw an eagle perched in the tree above them. The eagle admitted at once that he was the cause of the trouble.

'But if you will agree to share your meal with me, I will stop playing tricks and the ox will soon be roasted,' he screeched.

As the ox was a large one, Odin, Hoenir and Loki agreed to the eagle's suggestion, thinking there was plenty for all of them to eat. Then the flames of the fire leapt high and, in a few seconds, the meat was roasted.

Odin cut the carcass into juicy pieces and the gods were about to eat when the eagle swooped down from the tree. To their indignation, he snatched up nearly all the meat and left only a few miserable scraps for the three ravenous travellers.

Flying into a rage, Loki snatched up a stick and tried to beat the eagle into dropping some of the food. But the eagle was really the mountain giant, Thiassi, in disguise and he possessed great magical powers. The stick stuck fast to the back of the eagle and to Loki's hands.

The eagle soared away into the air and the helpless god was dragged through the sky with his feet crashing against the tops of the trees. His arms felt as if they were being dragged from their sockets.

'Release me!' begged Loki.

'Not until you promise to do something for me,' screeched Thiassi. He swooped up and down and blundered through the trees so that Loki's suffering was increased.

'When I release you,' contined Thiassi, 'say nothing about this to the other gods. When you return to Asgard, I want you to lure Iduna out to walk in Midgard so that I can capture her and the casket of the golden apples of youth.'

Loki was horrified, but he was in such pain that he swore he would do as Thiassi demanded. Then Thiassi released him and he walked back through the forest to rejoin Odin and Hoenir. He told them nothing of his promise, and they were amazed that he had escaped from the eagle so easily. After a few days the three gods completed their journey and returned to Asgard.

It so happened that Iduna's husband, Bragi, was away from Asgard, and she was alone. He was travelling as a minstrel, playing a lute and singing his poetry to anyone who would listen.

Loki went to see Iduna and asked if she would give him one of her golden apples. Smiling, Iduna opened the magic casket and, taking out an apple, handed it to Loki. At once another apple appeared in the casket. The supply seemed as secure as ever.

Instead of eating the apple, Loki looked at it and turned it over and held it up to the light.

Iduna was puzzled. 'Is something wrong?' she asked.

'No,' replied cunning Loki, 'but I am amazed. I thought there were no other apples like these, yet only this morning I saw some just like them down in the land of men.'

At first Iduna laughed and would not believe him, but Loki seemed so certain that the apples he had seen were exactly the same as Iduna's that she agreed to go with him to look. Taking her casket of golden apples with her, so that she might compare them, Iduna followed Loki outside the walls of Asgard.

Loki led her further and further from the safety of Asgard, then suddenly he hid and Iduna was alone. Now she realized that she had been tricked and turned to run back to Asgard, but she was too late. The giant Thiassi, still disguised as an eagle, swept down from the sky. Seizing her in his talons, he carried Iduna and the casket of apples away to his home in the mountains.

Loki slunk back to Asgard and told nobody about what had happened.

At first Iduna was not missed. Everyone thought that she had gone with her husband Bragi. Then gradually the effect of the golden apples began to wear off. Lines appeared on the beautiful young faces and hair began to turn white. The Aesir fell sick and ached with the pains of age. They searched for Iduna throughout Asgard, but they could not find her. They questioned each other and found that Iduna had last been seen in Loki's company.

Odin sent for Loki, who was so frightened that he confessed how he had betrayed Iduna to Thiassi. All the gods were furious and they threatened Loki with instant death if he did not rescue Iduna and get back the golden apples of youth.

Loki was growing old himself so he knew he would have to overcome his fear of Thiassi. He begged Freya, the goddess of love, to lend him her falcon disguise.

'Dressed as a falcon, Thiassi will not recognize me, and I can rescue Iduna more easily,' pleaded Loki.

So Freya lent Loki her falcon feathers and he flew off to the giants' mountain home. Fortunately, Thiassi was away fishing in the north and Iduna was sitting alone with the casket of apples at her side.

Loki circled around the sad and lonely goddess as she sat in the castle and transformed her and the casket into a small nut. Grasping this in his claws, he flapped his wings and flew as fast as he possibly could towards the safety of Asgard's walls.

But he did not escape unnoticed. Thiassi returned from fishing in time to see the falcon fleeing towards the horizon. Recognising the falcon's feathers as a disguise of the gods, he swiftly pulled on his own eagle's wings and flew in pursuit.

The huge eagle easily gained on the smaller falcon. Loki, weakened by old age, had to strain every muscle and summon up all his strength to keep ahead. At last he flapped exhausted over the walls of Asgard and fell to the ground.

Meanwhile the anxious gods had lined up along the walls of their lovely city, staring intently up into the sky to watch for Loki's return. Seeing the eagle pursuing him, they piled up wood shavings on the ramparts. As soon as Loki had swept over the walls to safety, the Aesir lit the wood and Thiassi was caught in the flames and smoke. Choking and blinded, he fell to the ground inside Asgard and was swiftly killed by the angry gods.

Loki and Iduna returned to their true shape and the gods were able to eat the golden apples of youth once more. How sweet they tasted. How happy the gods were to see their wrinkles and grey hair disappear and their youth and loveliness return.

'No wonder that the giants try such tricks to obtain the apples for themselves,' said Odin.

He ordered that Thiassi's eyes should be taken up into the heavens and turned into shimmering stars, so he would be remembered. The respect shown to the dead giant softened the anger of his brothers, and they caused no more trouble.

2

Perseus the Hero

Greece is a small country of mountains and islands lying in the south-east corner of Europe. According to legend, the gods of Ancient Greece lived on Mount Olympus. They married and quarrelled and suffered from jealousy just as humans do. The gods were always interfering in human affairs. They helped people they were fond of and punished anyone who offended them.

Long ago a man called Acrisius ruled the small Greek kingdom of Argos. One day he went to visit an ancient oracle, taking gifts for the priestess. He hoped she would give him a prophecy of health and prosperity, but instead she told him that he would die at the hand of his own grandson.

Shaking with fear, Acrisius hurried home. He ordered a brass tower to be built, and in it he imprisoned his only child, his daughter Danae. 'She will stay there for the rest of her life. I will not allow her to marry, and then I will have no grandson to kill me,' he said.

However, Acrisius had reckoned without the power of the gods. Zeus, the King of the gods, looked down from Mount Olympus and saw the beautiful princess alone in the brass tower. He flew down and, disguising himself as a shower of gold, entered the tower and took Danae as his human wife. Soon a little son, named Perseus, was born. Four years went by, but Acrisius knew nothing of the happiness that now filled the lonely tower.

Then one day, as the King was walking past, he heard a child's voice calling from the high windows. Filled with suspicion, he rushed into the tower and up the steps to the chamber where his daughter lived. There, before his horrified gaze, sat a lovely little boy playing with golden toys.

'Who is this?' screamed Acrisius, turning to Danae.

The frightened girl snatched Perseus up in her arms. 'He is my son,' she replied. As Acrisius reached out to seize the boy, she went on, 'He is the son of Zeus and you harm him at your peril.'

Acrisius went white with fury. He stared at his daughter and the grandson who was destined to kill him. How he longed to snatch the child and dash his brains out on the stone floor. But fear of Zeus stopped him.

Dragging Danae and the boy with him, he called his servants and rushed to the seashore. There he put Danae and little Perseus into a wooden chest and ordered his servants to push it out to sea. The swift currents would carry the chest far from land.

'I have not harmed a hair of their heads,' he growled. 'I have cast them out into the hands of fate. If Zeus cares for them so much, let him save them. They are his problem now, not mine. I hope they die, but if they survive, let it be many years before they find their way back to Argos.'

Acrisius turned his back on the shore and returned to his palace. For years he heard no word of his daughter and he thought that Danae and her child were dead.

The great god Zeus was not a faithful lover. Already the beauty of other maidens had caught his eye. However, he heard Danae's prayers as she drifted, hungry and thirsty, across the sea. Zeus ordered Poseidon, god of the oceans, to calm the heaving waves and to carry the wooden chest containing Danae and Perseus to the island of Seriphus. This island was ruled by King Polydectes.

Dictys, the brother of the king, was fishing from the rocks when the wooden chest came bobbing ashore. Dictys found the exhausted mother and child and took them to the royal palace, but it was Polydectes who fell in love with Danae and married her. Perseus became the stepson of a king and was brought up as a prince. Seeing Danae and Perseus so well settled in the world, Zeus turned his attention elsewhere. And so the years went by.

With a beautiful princess and a god as parents, Perseus grew up to be a beautiful and charming young man. He became friends with Athena, the goddess of wisdom. She persuaded another god, Mercury, to help her guide Perseus along the path of good fortune.

One day Polydectes said to Perseus, 'You are a young man of ability and yet you have no achievements to boast about. If you are to impress the rulers of this world, you must perform some great deed.'

Danae, Perseus and the whole court agreed that this was true. After much discussion they decided that Perseus should set out to kill Medusa, one of the Gorgons, by cutting off her head. If he could accomplish this, his fame would spread around the world.

The Gorgons were three sisters who lived in the underworld. Their job was to guard evil people who, after their death, had been sentenced to eternal torture.

Medusa was the only one of the three who was mortal. Once a beautiful golden-haired girl, she had offended the goddess Athena. In revenge Athena had transformed each lock of the girl's golden hair into a snake. Medusa's lovely eyes had become bloodshot yellow and the skin of her face had turned to livid green. Wings grew out of her scaly body. Her hands were hardened brass and her teeth were like those of a wild boar.

Perseus knew that killing Medusa would give him the reputation for which he longed. He also knew that it would be no easy task. Anyone who looked at Medusa was turned to stone. The young man asked Athena and Mercury for help.

'To slay the Gorgon,' said Athena, 'you will need a pair of winged sandals, a magic wallet in which to keep the head and the helmet of invisibility. Mercury will lend you a pair of his winged sandals, but the helmet and wallet are in the possession of nymphs. The three Grey Sisters, who live far away on the shores of the great sea, are the only ones who know where the nymphs can be found.'

Perseus set out at once to visit the Grey Sisters, guided by Athena and Mercury. The sisters were sitting together. With only a single eye and a single tooth between the three of them, they had to hand them to each other so that each could have a turn to see or to eat.

'Grey Sisters, please tell me where to find the nymphs who

20

keep the magic wallet and helmet of invisibility,' called Perseus.

The three Grey Sisters cackled with laughter. 'Why should we help you?' they screeched. 'Do not bother us, young man.'

Silently Perseus crept closer to the Grey Sisters. When one of them was wearing their single eye, he stood still. When they passed the eye from hand to hand, and for a moment could not see, he crept forward once more. At last he made a sudden dash and snatched both the eye and the tooth. Now the Sisters could neither see nor eat.

'Tell me where to find the nymphs who keep the magic wallet and the helmet of darkness,' called Perseus, 'or you will starve in blindness for the rest of your short days.'

Frantically the Grey Sisters groped about them. 'Have you the eye? Have you the tooth?' they screeched to one another.

'Scramble about as much as you like,' called Perseus. 'You will not find what you are looking for. I have your eye and your tooth and I will not return them until you tell me what I want to know.'

Then, grumbling and whining, the Grey Sisters told Perseus how to reach the nymphs. With a smile of triumph, he threw the eye and the tooth between the sisters' six searching hands and ran off. He was far away before any one of the weird creatures could fit the eye into her forehead and look round to find him.

The nymphs knew very well that Perseus was under Athena's protection. They gave him the magic wallet and the helmet of darkness. Mercury gave Perseus a sickle-shaped sword with which to cut off Medusa's head, and lent him a pair of winged sandals. Athena gave him a burnished shield.

'Listen to me carefully, young Perseus,' said Athena. 'You must not look at Medusa's face, or you will be turned to stone. When you reach the Gorgons' lair, hold my burnished shield high above your head. Find your way by looking at the reflection in the shield. When you see Medusa, strike her head from her shoulders with Mercury's sword. Put the head into the magic wallet and flee before the other Gorgons can kill you.'

Perseus thanked Athena and Mercury for their help. He strapped the winged sandals to his feet and, carefully holding the helmet, wallet, shield and sickle-shaped sword, flew swiftly to the Gorgons' lair. As he approached he saw many statues of men who had been turned to stone by Medusa's glare.

Perseus put the helmet on so that he became invisible and hovered in the air over the sleeping Gorgons. He slung the wallet on his shoulder and grasped the sickle-shaped sword in his right

hand. With his left hand he raised the burnished shield high above his head and tilted it towards the ground. In its glittering surface Perseus saw a reflection of the three frightful Gorgons.

Medusa's face glowed a livid green. Even though she slept, the snakes on her head slithered about and heaved in coils round her shoulders. Fearing that she might wake and turn him to stone, Perseus struck immediately. He severed Medusa's head with one clean slash of Mercury's sword. Groping behind him, still not daring to look directly at the Gorgon with his own eyes, Perseus put the severed head into the wallet and pulled the thongs closed. He sighed with relief. The terrible head was safe. A glance in the wrong direction could no longer turn him to stone.

Suddenly there was a great rustling of wings, and a huge winged horse, ridden by a fearsome warrior, sprang from the neck of the slaughtered Medusa. The horse flapped its wings and pounded its hooves among the stone statues of the Medusa's victims. The warrior shouted to the other Gorgons, 'Your sister has been killed. Wake up and take your revenge!'

The two living sisters opened their eyes, saw their sister's body and screamed with rage. Flapping their wings and rattling their scales they rose into the air, slashing and striking with their claws in all directions. 'Who has done this? Fight us too,' they screeched in their harsh voices.

Perseus pulled the helmet of invisibility more firmly onto his head. Clutching the wallet containing the Gorgon's head, he let the winged sandals carry him far away from that dreadful place. The Gorgons screamed and raged, but Perseus was protected by the gods. The helmet had hidden him and he escaped.

Perseus was so horrified by what had happened that he fled for many hours over the desert, for as long as his strength lasted. As he went, drops of the Gorgon's blood fell from the wallet on to the hot sand. They turned into the poisonous snakes that swarm over Africa to this day.

At last, when he was weak with tiredness, Perseus came to the kingdom of the giant Atlas. Clutching his precious possessions, the young man asked for shelter.

Atlas was suspicious. He owned an orchard where the trees produced apples of pure gold. Many people had visited him, only to try to rob him. He looked at the dishevelled, blood-streaked and exhausted Perseus. He looked at the glittering helmet in his hand, the burnished shield and the winged sandals on which the young man had descended from the skies. Most of all he looked at

the blood-stained sword and
the leather wallet from which
dripped blood that turned into wriggling snakes.

'And who might you be?' asked Atlas.

'I am Perseus, the son of Zeus,' replied Perseus, longing for
rest and food and not wanting to be questioned at length. 'I have
slain Medusa, the Gorgon, and I have her head in this wallet.'

Then, as Atlas showed no sign of offering him food or a bed,
Perseus added in a threatening voice, 'I have only to show the
Gorgon's head to my enemies for them to be turned to stone. It is
better for those I meet to be my friends.'

Atlas thought of his golden apples and of how easy it would be
for this young man to steal them. 'I will send him on his way
before he finds out the apples are here,' thought Atlas.

'I have no rooms, nor food fit to offer the son of a god,' said
Atlas. 'You had better fly on and look for shelter elsewhere.'

Perseus was furious. 'You miserable old man!' he shouted. 'All
I ask for is simply food and rest. If you will not give me that, then
you will never give anything to anyone.'

Looking away, he took Medusa's head from the wallet and held
it up in front of Atlas. The giant could not resist staring at the
monster he had heard so much about. He gazed and gazed, and
never stopped for he had turned to stone. His beard and hair
became forests, his arms and legs became great rocks. He turned

into the Atlas Mountains that stand in North Africa to this day.

Perseus put the head back into the wallet. He ate and drank and rested in Atlas's home. Next day, when he had recovered from the strain of his adventure, he flew onward. After a long journey across the desert, he came to Aethiopia, the kingdom of King Cepheus.

This land was in great trouble. The King's wife, Cassiopea, had boasted that her daughter Andromeda was more beautiful than the sea nymphs, who were known as the Nereides.

Furious with wounded pride, for Andromeda was very lovely and there was truth in Cassiopea's boast, the Nereides asked Poseidon, the god of the oceans, to punish the whole kingdom. Floods and storms were sent to devastate the land and a huge monster rose up from the sea and ate everybody who was not fast enough to run away from it.

'These terrible disasters can only be the work of the gods,' said King Cepheus. 'I will consult the oracle of Jupiter-Ammon in the Libyan desert to find out how we have offended them and what we must do to placate them.'

He returned to his kingdom white-faced and distraught. 'You have offended Poseidon with your boasting,' he said to his wife. 'The Nereides are jealous of Andromeda's beauty. The sea-monster will continue to raid our shore unless we offer Andromeda to him.'

As Perseus circled over the seashore of Aethiopia he saw the beautiful Andromeda chained to a rock with the waves washing round her feet.

The King and his court stood on the clifftops, making no move to help the unfortunate girl Perseus landed and asked why no one was helping the young woman who was chained down before the rising waves.

'There is nothing I wish more than to save my beloved only child,' groaned King Cepheus. 'But a terrible monster will only stop raiding my land if he is given my daughter as his prey.'

Perseus had fallen in love with Andromeda. 'I have slain the Gorgon,' he said.

'Why should I be frightened of a mere monster of the sea? If I slay this creature and save your child, will you give me her hand in marriage and let me take her to my home in Greece?'

'Yes! Anything! Save her! Save her!' gasped the desperate King.

Perseus put on his magic helmet and grasped Mercury's sword in his hand. Rising into the air on the winged sandals he flew towards the approaching beast. It heaved its huge head out of the waves and opened its jaws. Just as it was about to tear Andromeda to pieces the invisible Perseus killed it with a single blow. Then Perseus released Andromeda from the rock and carried her to the shore.

The wedding was arranged immediately. King Cepheus gave a feast in the great hall of the palace. The guests were toasting the happy couple when suddenly the door flew open and the warrior, Phineas, and his armed followers strode into the room. Phineas confronted Perseus.

'This marriage cannot take place,' he said. 'Andromeda was betrothed to me. Contract were signed. She cannot be your wife.'

Perseus stood up. 'And where were you when Andromeda was chained to the rock and the monster was rising out of the waves?' he asked. 'I did not see you then, nor did I hear you talking about marriage contracts. I saved Andromeda and she is mine.'

King Cepheus interrupted. 'Let us talk this over,' he said. 'Perhaps it would be better if Andromeda did not marry Perseus. After all, none of us knows anything about him and Greece is a long way away. The marriage arrangements with Phineas were beneficial to the kingdom. Let Andromeda marry Phineas and Perseus can take some other reward. I am sure we can easily find something. A chest of gold perhaps? Or we have some very nice jewellery that Perseus might like to take to his mother.'

Perseus was furious at such a suggestion. 'Are you trying to buy off a son of Zeus with necklaces and bracelets?' he shouted. 'I killed the monster in order to win Andromeda in marriage and I shall marry her.'

He drew his sword and rushed at Phineas. Phineas drew his sword and fought back. He was supported by his followers, and by King Cepheus's soldiers. Even a hero like Perseus could not win against such odds. Stepping back, he picked up the blood-stained wallet. 'Anyone who is my friend, look away,' he shouted.

He dragged Medusa's head out of the bag and waved it high in the air. His enemies were turned to stone but Andromeda, who loved him and so looked away, was saved.

The next day Perseus and his lovely bride sailed for Seriphus in Greece. Danae, his mother, welcomed him back with open arms. Perseus gave Medusa's head to Athena to thank her for her kindness. She fixed the head in the centre of her burnished shield and used it against her enemies.

Perseus and Andromeda lived happily together. One day Perseus said to his mother, 'Now I have proved my worth by killing Medusa, the Gorgon, I want to return to Argos to claim my inheritance from Acrisius.'

Danae nodded, but she told Perseus to be careful. 'A priestess prophesied that my father would be killed by his grandson,' she said. 'Acrisius will fear you and might even do you harm.'

'This is nonsense,' laughed Perseus. 'I do not want to kill the old man. That priestess must have misunderstood the oracle and given him the wrong prophecy.'

Perseus returned to Argos and asked to see his grandfather, King Acrisius. The old King fled in fear and took shelter with King Teutemias of Larissa. Perseus followed his grandfather, because he wanted to make peace with him.

'Arrange some games,' he said to King Teutemias. 'Let my grandfather watch me secretly and see that I am not a monster, but a worthy grandson.'

On the day of the games, Perseus entered the contest for throwing the discus. Acrisius watched from among the crowd of royal courtiers. He saw his grandson step forward and swing his arm. Then Perseus seemed to trip. He threw awkwardly and the discus flew over the crowd. It struck Acrisius on the head and he fell down dead. So, through no wish of his own, Perseus killed his grandfather. The prophesy had come true.

Perseus was distraught with grief. He held a lavish funeral for Acrisius and returned to Argos. However, he could not be happy in a kingdom that he had inherited in such a tragic way, so he exchanged kingdoms with King Megapenthes of Tiryns. He lived there with Andromeda for the rest of his life.

3

Beowulf

The Angles and the Saxons were among the many tribes that spread across northern Europe after the collapse of the Roman Empire in the fifth century. Some of them crossed over the sea from north-western Germany and settled in Britain, bringing with them their traditional tales. Beowulf is set in Denmark. It is one of the oldest poems in the English language. A manuscript of the poem survives in the British Library in London.

The centuries that followed the withdrawal of the Roman armies from northern Europe were known as the Dark Ages. Many small kingdoms fought among themselves. Those with well-trained fighting men conquered other tribes and gained more territory. In those days strong, brave warriors were admired as heroes. Beowulf is the story of just such a hero.

Hrothgar was King of Denmark. He had a well-trained army of fighting men and the people of Denmark lived in peace. No one dared to attack land defended by Hrothgar and his warriors. To reward his men, Hrothgar built a magnificent hall where they could meet together and feast during the dark days of winter. A hall where they could talk of past battles, and plan what they should do if an enemy attacked in the future.

As time went by Hrothgar began to grow old. But still young men still came to train with him and the kingdom remained safe. Then danger threatened in a way that no one had foreseen. Hrothgar and his men were helpless.

Hrothgar's great hall was called Heorot. It stood on the edge of some lonely marshes. A dreadful monster named Grendel came to live in these marshes with his mother. Their home was a dank cave below a dark pool. The terrible pair were so frightful that even the wild animals dared not approach them.

One night, while wandering across the marshes in search of an unwary animal or a traveller to eat, Grendel heard laughter and music coming from Heorot. Creeping closer, he saw the warriors and King Hrothgar enjoying themselves and he was jealous of their happiness. He waited until the small hours of the morning when the men were asleep around the firepit. Then, protecting himself with a magic mist that no weapon could pierce, he crept into Heorot. Before anyone realised what was happening Grendel slew thirty of the warriors and dragged them away to his lair. In the morning, when the survivors woke up, they saw the bloodstains on the floor and knew that this was Grendel's work.

The next night the same thing happened. Grendel crept unseen and unheard into Heorot. He killed another thirty warriors and took their bodies away. The bravest of Hrothgar's men tried to defend the hall against the wicked fiend, but Grendel was not easily seen and even less easily caught. The magic mist protected him from swords and knives. Soon no warriors would dare to feast in Hrothgar's hall and the old King sat alone.

Beowulf, the son of Hrothgar's sister, lived in Geatland, in the south of what is now Sweden. Beowulf was brave, strong and well-trained in fighting, but he was young and needed experience against other foes. He heard about Grendel and thought this would be a good challenge. Beowulf gathered together a band of friends and they set out to fight the monster. Whatever happened, they would gain glory and, if they survived, they would have learned new skills with which to defend their own people.

Beowulf and his companions sailed across the straits to the shores of Denmark. They strode up from the beach to the forlorn grandeur of Heorot and stood before the King.

'Hrothgar,' said Beowulf, bowing low. 'I have come to rid your hall of this fiend, Grendel, who comes silently in the night. I have slain giants and I have slain sea-monsters. I am not frightened of this creature.'

Hrothgar welcomed his brave young guest, but shook his head sadly. 'I hope you will succeed where others have failed,' he said, 'but do not be too confident. Grendel creeps in unseen. Weapons are no use against him. I fear for your life, young man.'

But Beowulf felt no fear. That night he and his men feasted with Hrothgar in Heorot. When the meal was over, Hrothgar went away. Even he no longer dared pass the night in the hall. Then Beowulf laid aside his sword and took off his coat of mail.

'If Grendel likes to fight without a weapon, then I will oblige him,' said Beowulf to his men. They settled down to rest, each wondering to himself if he would ever see his home again.

In the darkness before dawn, Grendel came stalking across the marshes. He arrived at the door of Heorot and although it was locked with iron bars, forced his way in. He strode between the

tables, his eyes glowing red with anticipation at the sight of so many warriors to slay. Seizing a young man, he killed him with one blow. Then he reached for Beowulf.

Grendel felt his arm grasped in the strongest grip that he had ever felt. He knew at once that he had met his match and tried to run away, but Beowulf jumped to his feet and seized Grendel's arm in an even tighter hold.

Grendel cried out in pain. He struggled and wrenched at his arm in an effort to escape. The hall shook with their thrashing and struggling. At last, with a scream that no one who heard it would ever forget, Grendel wrenched his body away from his arm. With blood pouring from his gaping shoulder, he staggered away through the marshes. But he never reached his lair. Beowulf was left in the great hall, clutching the frightful, severed arm.

In the morning, when the sky was light, Beowulf and his friends followed the trail of blood across the marshes and found Grendel's body. Leaving the body where it lay, Beowulf returned to spread the good news. There was much rejoicing and everyone congratulated the brave young man. King Hrothgar gave Beowulf and his men many fine presents and Hrothgar's warriors returned to sleep in the hall. Beowulf and his men were lodged in another house, ready to leave for home the next day.

But Grendel's mother had also found his body and was mad with grief. Thirsting for revenge, she strode into Heorot that night and entered the hall while the warriors slept. She seized a young man who was very dear to Hrothgar and slew him, screaming that she would have revenge. Then, in the confusion that followed, she slipped away to the cave under the lake.

In the morning Beowulf was told the dreadful news that now another monster had killed some of Hrothgar's warriors. Again he showed no fear, but offered to go to the lake and kill Grendel's mother, as he had killed the fiend himself.

Hrothgar ordered horses to be saddled and rode out over the marshes with Beowulf and a band of men until they reached the dark pool that had been Grendel's home.

Beowulf stared down into the murky water and swore that it would not stop him from reaching Grendel's mother and slaying her. He put on his coat of mail and his helmet. Then he took up his sword and dived into the cold water. He groped about in the black water until suddenly he felt himself seized in a powerful grip. Grendel's mother had found him!

With amazing strength, Grendel's monstrous mother dragged

Beowulf into a damp cave. To his surprise, he saw that it was lit by a beam of white fire. Now Beowulf could see his enemy and, wrenching himself free, he struck at her with his sword. But Grendel's mother was also protected by a magic mist and could not be harmed by a sword made by human hands. The sword broke into pieces.

Flinging Beowulf to the ground, Grendel's mother pulled out a dagger and was about to stab him, when the young man saw a beautiful sword hanging on the wall. He recognised it as the magic giant's sword called Hrunting. With one last effort, he rolled across and reached up. He snatched the sword from its scabbard and with one blow cut off the head of the monster.

Beowulf got to his feet panting. He looked round the cave and saw Grendel's body lying on a couch. With a final slash of the sword he cut Grendel's head from his body. But then a strange thing happened. Grendel's poisoned blood melted the blade of the sword so that only the jewelled hilt remained in Beowulf's hand.

Carrying the two heads, and the jewelled hilt of the ancient sword, Beowulf left the cave and swam to the surface of the pool. How joyfully he was welcomed by the anxious group waiting on the shore. The heads of Grendel and his mother were taken back to Heorot for everyone to see. Beowulf presented King Hrothgar with the jewelled hilt and Hrothgar, in gratitude, gave Beowulf and his men more fine presents before they sailed home.

4
Aesop's Fables

The most famous fables are these told by a Greek called Aesop, who lived in the sixth century BC. Aesop has been described as a slave who later gained his freedom and became an adviser to kings. But it is more likely that the name Aesop was invented to provide an author for hundreds of short, sharply-observed fables.

Mercury and the Woodman

One day a woodman was cutting down trees by a river. Suddenly his axe hit a hard spot in a tree-trunk. The axe flew from his hands and fell into the water. The woodman was standing on the bank of the river moaning about his loss, when Mercury, the messenger of the gods, appeared before him.

'Why are you so upset?' asked the god.

When the woodman explained that he had lost the axe with which he made his living, Mercury took pity on him and dived into the river. Presently he came to the surface with a gold axe in his hand.

'Is this yours?' he asked the woodman.

'No,' the man replied.

Again Mercury dived to the bottom of the river and this time he came up with a silver axe in his hand.

'Is this silver axe yours?' he asked.

'No, that is not mine either,' replied the woodman.

For a third time Mercury dived beneath the water and this time he came up with the woodman's plain axe.

'That is mine. Oh, thank you, sir!' smiled the woodman, eagerly reaching out his hands to take it.

Mercury was so impressed with the man's honesty that he gave him not only his own axe, but also the gold and silver axes as well. The woodman hurried home to tell his friends of his good fortune because the gold and silver axes were worth a great deal of money.

The woodman's friends congratulated him on his luck. However, one of the men was envious and decided to see if he also could become rich too. He went to the river bank with his axe and, after a little banging and cutting at a tree, he dropped his axe into the river. Then he stood at the water's edge and wept and wailed. At once the god Mercury stood before him and asked him what was upsetting him.

When the man said that he had lost his axe in the water, Mercury dived down and came up waving a gold axe in his hand.

'Is this yours?' he asked.

'Yes! Yes! That is mine. Give it to me,' said the man, reaching forward and trying to snatch the axe from Mercury's hand.

Mercury was so disgusted by the man's dishonesty that he refused either to give him the gold axe, or to retrieve the man's own axe from the river.

Honesty is the best policy.

Belling the Cat

Once upon a time a group of mice met to hold a discussion. A big, clever cat had come to live in the same house. How could they protect themselves from attack?

Many ideas were put forward. At last one mouse said, 'I think I have the perfect solution. We must get hold of a bell, which I know how to do, and then we must hang the bell round the cat's neck. Whenever the cat moves, the bell will ring. So we will always be warned when she is creeping close to attack us.'

'Wonderful! Marvellous!' cheered the other mice. 'That is a brilliant idea. A bell must be hung round the cat's neck. Why did no one think of that before? Our troubles are over.'

Everyone thanked the mouse who had made the suggestion and he was given some extra grain.

Among all the cheers and murmurs of approval, a little voice, belonging to a small, unimportant mouse, was heard asking, 'But who will hang the bell round the cat's neck?'

There was a silence that grew longer and longer. Then there was a shuffling of feet. All the mice suddenly remembered important engagements that they had to hurry to. No one ever mentioned the idea of belling the cat again.

The Wolf and the Lamb

A hungry wolf came upon a lamb that had strayed from the flock. He wanted to eat the little creature but, knowing it to be blameless and innocent, tried to find an excuse for such a cruel action.

'Aren't you the lamb that insulted me last year?' he asked.

'No,' bleated the lamb. 'Last year I wasn't even born.'

'Then you have wronged me by eating in my pastures,' growled the wolf.

'That is not possible,' baa-ed the lamb. 'I have not yet started to eat grass.'

'Well, I am sure you have done me a bad turn somehow,' snapped the wolf. 'I know. You have fouled my drinking water by drinking from my stream.'

'I have not touched your drinking water,' wailed the lamb. 'I have drunk nothing but my mother's milk.'

At that the wolf lost patience and killed the lamb and ate it.

'I'm hungry. That is a good enough excuse,' he said.

The Goose that laid the Golden Eggs

A man and his wife owned a goose that laid a solid gold egg every day. But they were not satisfied with their good fortune and complained that they were not growing rich quickly enough.

'If we cut the goose open, we can have all the eggs at once,' they thought. 'Why should we wait for only one a day?'

They killed the goose and slit it open, only to find that it was just like other geese inside. There was no store of golden eggs.

So the man and his wife did not become rich quickly and, as their goose was now dead, they also lost the daily egg they had been getting. Through their greed, they had lost everything.

The Fox and the Grapes

One fine day a hungry fox was hurrying through a garden when he saw a bunch of ripe grapes hanging from a trellis against a sunny wall. Wishing to eat the grapes, the fox jumped into the air and snapped at the fruit. He scratched and pawed at the vine, but try as he might, he could not reach the grapes.

In the end the fox walked out of the garden with an angry toss of his head. 'I thought those grapes were ripe,' he snarled, 'but now I see they are sour.'

The Oak and the Reeds

A tall oak tree grew on the bank of a river. It held its head proudly up to the sky and looked down with scorn on the reeds, so thin and small below. Then one day there was a strong wind that uprooted the tall oak tree and cast it to the ground.

The oak tree lay in the mud feeling bewildered and sorry for itself. It said to the reeds, 'How is it that you, who are so weak and thin, are undamaged, while I, who am strong, have been destroyed?'

'Aaah,' murmured the reeds, swaying in the breeze. 'You stood tall and strong and stubborn and fought against something more powerful than yourself. We lesser beings bow and yield before every wind that blows and the wrath of the storm passes harmlessly over our heads.'

5

How Finn Found Bran

Ireland was never conquered by the Roman legions, and its Celtic traditions survived intact. The Irish have always been good story-tellers. Finn was a great hero and there are many stories about his battles and daring deeds.

Long, long ago, in the days when Corm MacArt was King of Ireland, there was a band of soldiers known as the Feni of Erin. They were tall and bold, and so fearless that no enemy could stand against them; even their friends were afraid of them.

The captain of these fearless men was Finn, the son of Cumhal, whose castle stood on the Hill of Allen. This hill is quite close to Kildare, that lies to the south-west of Dublin. Finn was the bravest of the brave. He was an awesome sight when he was in the middle of a fight, waving his magic sword, with his long hair streaming down his back.

If people were afraid of Finn, they were terrified of his faithful dog. Bran was huge and tireless, and had long, snapping teeth. He had one claw that was much sharper than the rest, and it was poisonous. A scratch from the claw never healed, but festered until the unfortunate victim died.

Mostly Finn kept a golden shoe tied over this lethal claw but, when he found himself in danger he would call Bran and take off the shoe. Bran would fly at his master's enemies, and very few had the courage to stand and face him. Some people wondered where such a dog came from, but the old ones knew that Finn had stolen him from Faeryland. This is how it happened.

Times had been peaceful, which was unusual, and one day Finn decided to go walking, alone and unattended. He had not gone far when he met a man whose face was unfamiliar. This was strange, because Finn knew all the men who lived on his land.

'Who are you to be walking here?' asked Finn.

'I am a clever man in search of work,' replied the stranger.

'In what way are you clever?' asked Finn.

'I never sleep,' replied the man. 'A master must have a use for a man who is always awake.'

'That is true,' smiled Finn. 'Follow me and I will employ you.'

Hardly had Finn taken another step, when he was confronted by a second stranger. 'Who are you who walks so boldly over my land?' asked Finn.

'I am a clever man in search of work,' replied the stranger.

'In what way are you clever?' asked Finn.

'I can hear the slightest sound,' replied the man. 'I can even hear the grass growing from the ground.'

'Can you indeed?' smiled Finn. 'Then you had better follow me and I will employ you.' He did not immediately see the use of such a talent, but thought it better for the man to be working for him than for an enemy.

Scarcely a hundred yards further along the road, Finn met a third stranger. Again he asked the man what he was doing and again received the same reply – that he was a clever man looking for work. This stranger claimed that he was so strong that once he gripped something, no one could make him let go.

'In that case, join these other men and work for me,' said Finn.

Finn met four more men who, like the others, were invited to work for him. One was an expert thief, the next was a skilled climber, the third claimed he could throw a stone that would turn into a wall upon landing, and the fourth said he was such a fine marksman that he never missed a shot.

Now Finn was no fool and, with such unusual things happening to him one after the other, he rightly concluded that the faeries were at work, and perhaps to his advantage. So he strode onwards to see what the rest of the day would bring.

Looking around, it seemed to Finn that the landscape suddenly changed. He found himself close by a palace that was quite unknown to him. As night was falling, Finn knocked at the palace gate and asked for shelter for himself and his men. He was allowed into the palace and there he found the King and Queen in the deepest sorrow.

'Our first two sons were stolen by faeries or demons or some such creatures,' wept the King. 'Now another lovely baby has been born to us and we are afraid that this child will be stolen too.'

Then Finn thought he understood why he had met the seven strangers, and why their steps had led them to this palace.

'My men and I will guard your new baby,' he smiled. 'Have no more fear.'

Finn sent for the man who never slept and told him to watch the baby in its chamber. He told the man who could hear the grass growing to sit in the ante-chamber and listen for anyone coming. Finally, he told the man with the strong grip to sit by the baby's cradle.

'Whatever approaches,' said Finn, 'be it demon, monster or faery, seize it and never let it go.'

The King's household settled down for the night and at first everything was peaceful. Then, as midnight struck, the man sitting in the ante-chamber said, 'I feel so drowsy.'

'So do we,' yawned the courtiers who also sat in the ante-chamber. They were inquisitive to see what would happen.

The man who could hear the grass growing cocked his head and said, 'I can hear sweet music far off in the distance. It is coming nearer and nearer. Do you know what it can be?'

The courtiers' faces turned white with fear. 'It is the Master Harper,' they cried. 'His playing puts everyone to sleep long before he arrives. How can we guard the baby if we are asleep?'

The man sitting in the baby's chamber laughed and said, 'Nothing ever puts me to sleep. I will keep you all awake.' Getting to his feet, the man walked continually round the palace, shaking the guards and the courtiers so that no one slept.

This left the man with the strong grip sitting at the side of the cradle. Suddenly he saw a long, skinny arm come right through the wall and reach over to where the baby lay. 'Steal the child, would you?' roared the man. 'Well, you will be unlucky this time!'

Leaping to his feet he seized the mysterious hand. A terrible struggle followed in which the man was thrown all over the room. But he did not relax his grip and finally, with one mighty heave, he pulled the hand and arm from the unseen body.

The courtiers rushed forward to look at the weird trophy. In the excitement and jostling, no one noticed a second hand push through the wall and snatch up the baby. The baby cried with fright, but by then it was too late. By the time the courtiers realised what was happening the child was disappearing through the wall. Everyone rushed outside and searched in the darkness, but without success. The King and Queen were heartbroken.

No one was more distressed than Finn, who had failed to guard the baby as he had promised. He swore to the King that he would not rest until he had found the child again. Calling his seven men, he strode out of the palace and back to his home.

Near Finn's home, lying on the seashore, was a boat that had taken seven years and seven days to build. Taking his seven new servants with him, Finn launched the boat and they sailed until they reached a rocky shore. Pulling the boat well up the beach, Finn and his men walked inland until they came to a lonely house. Its walls were high and covered with slippery eel skins.

Finn called the man who was an expert climber. 'Climb to the top of that house. Put your eye to the chimney and tell me what you see,' he ordered.

The man had not boasted in vain. He climbed easily over the slippery eel skins and peered down the chimney. When he returned, he reported to Finn that a one-eyed giant, whose arm had been torn from his body, was sitting inside the house. In his remaining hand the giant held a baby. Two handsome boys were playing on the floor.

Finn knew he had found the stolen children. Turning to the man who had boasted of being an expert thief, Finn told him to go into the house and steal all three children.

Silently the thief lifted the latch of the door and crept into the house. Without a sound he picked up the two boys. Then gently, so that the giant did not realize what was happening, he took the baby from the enormous hand.

He turned to go but, on the way to the door, he saw three puppies playing among the rushes on the floor. Being a thief, he could not resist taking the little dogs as well. Thus laden, he tiptoed out to rejoin Finn and the others.

Carrying the children, the eight men turned and ran for

the shore. They had not gone far before they heard loud barking. Looking back, they saw a huge tawny hound, with eyes glowing like lamps, bounding after them. It was the puppies' mother.

'Now it is your turn to work,' said Finn, turning to the man who had boasted he could throw a stone that would turn into a wall as soon as it hit the ground.

As the men ran hard for the shore, the stone-thrower picked up stone after stone and threw them behind him. As each stone struck the ground, a wall rose up, but this did not stop the mother dog. She bounded on after her puppies.

'Throw down a puppy for her,' shouted Finn. For a moment the dog paused to sniff happily at the little creature. But then she bounded on in pursuit.

'Throw down another,' panted Finn, and this time the mother was satisfied because she stayed behind with her two puppies.

Finn and his men reached their boat and thankfully dragged it into the sea. They rowed for many hours. When they were within sight of the shores of Ireland, they thought themselves safe at last, and rested on their oars. But when they looked back they saw a terrifying sight. A ball of light flashed and darted in the water. All around it, the sea foamed and frothed as if someone were beating it into a fury.

One of the servants called, 'It is the giant. I can see his great face with his one eye glaring.'

Finn turned to the man who was a fine marksman and said, 'Now is the time to show us how good you are with a bow.'

The man pulled the bowstring back to his ear and sent an arrow flying straight and true into the terrible eye. The giant threw his remaining arm high into the air, crashed back into the sea and disappeared from sight. He was never heard of again.

Finn and his men hurried to the King's palace and restored the children to their delighted parents.

'What can I give you as a reward?' the King asked Finn.

'I want no reward,' smiled Finn, 'but I will keep the puppy, for I believe he has come from an enchanted land and will be a good friend to me in times of danger.'

So Finn set off to walk to his own home. On the way, strange to say, his seven servants went missing, but the puppy remained. So who can doubt that what the old people say is true and that the dog, which Finn called Bran, did come from Faeryland?

6

The Best Teacher

Romania, in eastern Europe, has beautiful mountains and forests. In the old days gypsies roamed the countryside and dashing noblemen rode their fine horses into battle. The Romanian people have a great sense of fun and many of their folktales are full of laughter.

Once upon a time, long ago, a man was blessed with a fine house, healthy animals and fertile land. This man was also fortunate enough to have a handsome, loving son. But the boy had never known anything but good times and had never had to deal with any sort of problem.

'The lad must have some experience of dealing with ill luck,' said his father.

From then on he gave his son all the awkward and difficult jobs to do. However, luck was with the young man until the day his father sent him into the forest to bring back timber. Only a rickety old cart was free for the work and the father watched his son harness two oxen to it.

If that cart breaks down today, then it will be good experience for the boy, he thought. The father smiled at his son. 'If that cart breaks up when you are alone in the forest, necessity will teach you what to do,' he said.

'Right you are, Father,' replied the lad, who was good and loyal, but not the cleverest young man in the world. He thought that Necessity must be some handyman who lived in the forest and helped travellers in trouble.

The son drove the oxen far into the forest where there were good trees suitable for felling. He worked hard, cutting down the trees, sawing them up and loading them on to the cart. When the cart was full, he collected the oxen from where they had been munching at the patches of forest grass, re-harnessed them and set off for home. However, as he drove over a patch of rough ground, the cart lurched and one of the axles broke.

'1 hope that Necessity fellow is nearby,' thought the son. He stood up and shouted, 'Necessity! NECESSITY!! NE–CESS–ITY!!!'

No one answered.

Then the young man ran up first one path, then another, always shouting at the top of his voice, 'NECESSITY! NE–CESS–ITY!!'

Still there was no reply.

The son became worn out. 'I will not bother searching for Father's clever friend any more,' he said. 'I will do the job myself. Father gave me useless advice.'

The young man went back to the cart, took off his coat, and unharnessed the oxen. He took some wood from the cart and mended the axle. Then he re-harnessed the oxen and drove home, having made a fine job of both the repair and of collecting good timber.

His father was pleased with him, but the boy was not pleased with his father.

'I could not find that fellow, Necessity, anywhere,' said the son. 'He did not teach me anything. All I learned was that if a job needs doing, it is best to do it myself, then it is done quickly and well. If I go looking for help from other people, I can look for ever.'

'There you are,' smiled the father. 'Necessity did teach you a good lesson. I told you he would.'

7
Lazy Jack

Lazy or Idle Jack is a popular character in English folklore.
He appears regularly in pantomimes every Christmas.

Once upon a time, there was a boy called Jack, who lived with his widowed mother in the rain-swept countryside of England. The mother earned a few coins by spinning wool, but Jack was lazy and earned nothing. At last the widow lost all patience with her son and told him that if he did not find some work, she would turn him out of the house to look after himself.

Dear me! thought Jack. What a terrible thing that would be! So he went and hired himself for the day to a farmer. The farmer gave him a penny and Jack was very pleased. However, on the way home, he dropped the penny into a stream and lost it.

'You stupid boy!' said his mother. 'You should have put the penny in your pocket.'

'You're right,' agreed Jack. 'That is what I shall do next time.'

The next day Jack went out and hired himself to a dairyman. At the end of the afternoon, Jack was given a jugful of creamy, warm milk. He put the jug into his pocket and walked back home.

'I did as you said, Mother,' called Jack, stepping indoors. But when he lifted the jug from his pocket, he found he had spilled all the milk on the way home.

'Where have you spent all your life?' groaned his mother. 'Don't you know you should have carried it on your head?'

'You're right,' agreed Jack. 'That is what I shall do next time.'

Two days later Jack hired himself to another farmer. In payment the farmer gave him a cream cheese. Jack put the cheese on his head and walked home. For once the sun was shining. The cheese melted and ran all over his shirt.

'You idiot!' shrieked his mother, who liked cream cheese. 'You should have carried it carefully in your hands.'

'You're right,' agreed Jack, who was nothing if not good-natured. 'That is what I shall do next time.'

On the next day Jack worked all day for a baker whose cat had recently given birth to kittens.

'Take a kitten for your payment, Jack,' smiled the baker.

Jack took the kitten and carried it carefully in his hands, but the kitten did not want to leave its mother and scratched Jack so much that he had to let it go. 'You fool!' said his mother, when Jack told her what had happened. 'You should have tied a piece of string around its neck and dragged it behind you.'

'You're right,' agreed Jack. 'That is what I shall do next time.'

The following day Jack hired himself to a butcher, who gave him a shoulder of lamb as payment. Jack took the meat, tied a piece of string around it and dragged it behind him all along the road. By the time he reached home, the meat was not fit to eat.

'You ninny!' sighed his mother. 'You certainly take after your father. You should have carried it on your shoulder.'

'You are so clever, Mother,' said Jack. 'I'll do that next time.'

On the following Monday, Jack hired himself to a cattle-keeper, who gave him a donkey in payment for his work. Now the donkey was heavy, but Jack was a strong lad. With much heaving and grunting on his part—and also that of the donkey—Jack pulled the donkey on to his shoulder and set off for home.

On the way he passed the home of a rich merchant who had a rather strange daughter. The girl had never laughed in her life and the doctors had said she would never be cheerful until she saw something she thought was funny. 'To think that I had to pay good money for advice like that,' moaned the merchant.

However, he was fond of his daughter and, wishing to see her happy, he promised her hand in marriage, and a fine dowry, to any young man who could make her laugh.

As luck would have it, the merchant's daughter was looking from her window as Lazy Jack stumbled past carrying the braying donkey. The girl had never seen anything so ridiculous in her life and she burst out laughing. The merchant was delighted. He ran into the street and, inviting Jack indoors, asked him if he would like to marry his daughter and accept a gift of money. Jack agreed and they lived happily together for the rest of their lives.

As Jack was a kind-hearted lad, he saw that his mother had everything she needed. 'My Jack may be lazy and stupid,' smiled his mother, 'but he managed to get it right when it mattered.'

8

The Sword in the Stone

Tales about King Arthur and his Knights of the Round Table go back to the Dark Ages. The Britons were probably the first people to tell stories of Arthur, and eventually they became popular all over Europe. In 1470 they were gathered together in a best-selling book, Le Morte D'Arthur, *by Sir Thomas Malory. Nowadays Arthur and his Knights of the Round Table are popularly shown living as kings and knights did in the days of Malory. However, historians think that Arthur was not a king, but a successful war chief, who lived and fought at the time of the first Anglo-Saxon invasions of Britain.*

Many hundreds of years ago Uther Pendragon was King of England. Those were troubled, warlike days. The King was always fighting and moving about the land. That was why, when a baby son was born to King Uther and his wife Igraine, the child was given to Merlin the magician to bring up in safety.

Merlin took the boy, called him Arthur, and put him in the care of a knight called Sir Ector. Sir Ector was not an important nobleman, but he was honest and kind. He already had a son, called Kay, and Arthur was brought up as Kay's younger brother.

In the usual way of things in those days, Arthur would have lived with Sir Ector until he was ten or twelve years old, and then returned to his father's court to be trained as a fighting prince.

However, barely two years after Arthur had been given to Merlin, King Uther died and the kingdom fell into chaos. The great dukes all fought one another and everyone fought the Anglo-Saxon invaders who were constantly attacking the people who lived near the coasts.

The few people who knew that the little Prince existed did not know where he was. Sir Ector knew that Arthur was the son of an important nobleman, but he did not realize that he was the son of King Uther. So the years went by, and Arthur lived happily on Sir

Ector's small estate deep in the country, while England was in turmoil because there was no strong king to keep order.

At last Merlin the magician visited the Archbishop of Canterbury and advised him to send for all the noblemen of the realm and all the knights to meet in London at Christmas.

'As our Lord Jesus was born by a miracle on that night, perhaps in His mercy, He will send us a miracle to show who should be King of this troubled kingdom,' said Merlin.

The Archbishop of Canterbury agreed and all the nobles and knights were called to meet in London by Christmas Day, or risk being put under the Church's curse. Just before Christmas, the nobles assembled at the great church of St Paul. They asked God to hear their prayers and to help them to choose a worthy king.

When they came out of the church, they saw an amazing sight. A huge stone stood in the middle of the churchyard where no stone had stood before. Embedded in the stone was an anvil of steel a foot high. Pushed into the anvil was a magnificent sword and written round the sword in gold were the words:

Whosoever pulleth out this sword of this stone,
is rightwise King born of all England.

Everyone was amazed. Some of the nobles ran to fetch the Archbishop. 'God has given us a sign,' he said. 'We must pray once more and then those who think they are fit to be King may try to pull the sword out of the stone.'

Many nobles tried to pull the sword from the stone, but none succeeded. 'The man who can claim the sword is not yet here,' said the Archbishop. 'God will send him. Meanwhile, let ten knights of good repute guard the sword.' So it was agreed.

Then Merlin the magician spoke secretly to the Archbishop again. 'A tournament should be arranged for New Year's Day,' he said. 'Otherwise those who have not succeeded in pulling the sword from the stone will become bored and go home. All the nobles must be here to acclaim the rightful King, when at last he is found. What is more, a tournament will attract many people. Surely the boy born to be King will be among them.'

The Archbishop of Canterbury agreed and so it was arranged.

Talk of the great meeting in London and the tournament on New Year's Day had reached the ears of Sir Ector living down in the country. He rode to London with his son, Sir Kay, who had been made a knight the previous November. Young Arthur, who was not yet old enough to be made a knight, rode as a squire to his brother, Sir Kay.

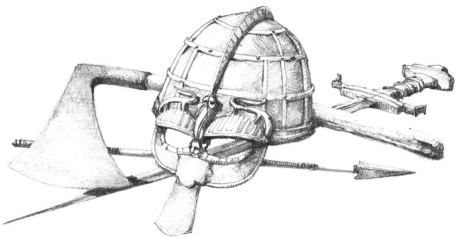

London was of course very crowded and Sir Ector had to take lodgings far out of the city. On the day of the great tournament, Sir Ector, Sir Kay and Arthur rode into town. Suddenly Sir Kay gasped in horror: 'Arthur! I have forgotten my sword. I cannot fight without it. Please go back to our lodgings and fetch it for me. If I ride back, I shall be tired before the tournament starts.'

'Very well,' agreed Arthur, who was a good-natured lad. In any case it was his duty as a squire to serve his brother.

Arthur rode back along the road as quickly as he could. When he reached the lodging house, he found to his dismay that it was locked and shuttered. 'The lady of the house has gone to watch the tournament,' called a child playing in a nearby field. 'There is no way of getting into that house until she returns tonight.'

Arthur rode back towards the jousting field in great dismay. Kay could not take part in the tournament without a sword. It was very upsetting. Then, as he rode past St Paul's, Arthur saw a magnificent sword sticking out of an anvil high on a huge stone.

Well, whoever owns that sword cannot want it very much if they leave it lying about like that, thought Arthur. If I can take it to Kay, he will have a fine sword to use in the tournament.

Tying up his horse, Arthur climbed on to the stone, seized hold of the sword with both his hands and pulled it from the anvil. Then, remounting his horse, he hurried to catch up with Sir Ector and Sir Kay. The sword Arthur held in his hands was, of course, the magic sword. It was unguarded because all the knights had gone to the jousting.

'Kay! Kay!' called Arthur, spurring up beside his brother. 'The lodging house was locked and I could not fetch your own sword, but I found this sword pushed in an anvil. Will it do for you?'

By this time, Sir Kay had been talking with other knights and nobles and he had heard all about the sword in the stone.

'Did you get this sword from St Paul's churchyard?' he asked.

'I'm not sure,' replied Arthur. 'It was outside a big church. But, if people leave good swords lying about pushed into stones, they deserve to lose them. It's your sword now, Kay. Take it and win.'

Kay was a good young man but for once the temptation was too great for him. He went to his father, Sir Ector, and showed him the sword. 'Father,' he said. 'I have the sword from the stone, therefore I must be King of England.'

Sir Ector looked at the sword and looked at his son. He knew his son had no right to be King. He took the sword and he and Sir Kay went back into St Paul's church. Arthur went with them, hoping he would not be scolded for taking the sword.

Sir Ector put a Bible into Sir Kay's hand and said, 'Now my son, tell me how you came by the sword.'

'Sir,' said Sir Kay, 'my brother, Arthur, gave it to me.'

Then Sir Ector asked Arthur, 'How did you get the sword?'

'I rode back to the lodging house, but it was locked so I could not bring Kay his sword,' said Arthur. 'As I rode past here, I saw this sword in the anvil in the stone. I thought that Kay need not be without a sword while this fine sword was lying unwanted in a churchyard. So I pulled it out of the stone and gave it to Kay. I...I am sorry if I have done wrong.'

Sir Ector looked hard at the boy he had brought up as his own. 'You have pulled the sword from the stone,' he said, 'and now you must be King of England.'

Arthur stared in amazement at the man he knew as his father. 'Me?' he said. 'Why should I be King of England?'

'Because God has willed it,' replied Sir Kay, 'and because you pulled the sword from the stone.'

'But it was easy,' said Arthur. 'Anyone could do it.'

'Really?' said Sir Ector. 'Then push it back in and let me try.'

Arthur climbed on to the huge stone and rammed the sword into the anvil. Sir Ector climbed up beside him and pulled and pulled at the handle of the sword, but he could not move it.

'You try, Kay,' said Sir Ector.

Kay scrambled up on to the stone and tried with both hands and all his strength to pull the sword free. He did not succeed.

'Now you try, Arthur,' said Sir Ector. His face and his voice were as serious as Arthur had ever seen.

Arthur put his hands round the sword and pulled it free easily. Then Sir Ector and Sir Kay knelt before the boy.

Arthur was distressed. 'Father! Kay! Why are you kneeling?'

'Arthur,' replied Sir Ector, 'I am not your father and Kay is not your brother. I knew you were of noble blood, but to tell the truth, I never dreamed that you were as high born as it seems you are.' Sir Ector told Arthur how he had been brought to him by Merlin and Arthur wept, because he loved Sir Ector and Sir Kay dearly.

'Even if I am to be King, you will not leave me, will you?' he asked, and Sir Ector and Sir Kay promised to stay with Arthur as long as he needed them.

Then the three of them went to the Archbishop of Canterbury and showed him the sword and told him what had happened.

On the next day the Archbishop called all the nobles together. Arthur put the sword back in the stone and anyone who wished tried to pull it out. No one succeeded. Only Arthur could take it.

Many of the great lords were angry and said it would shame them to be ruled by a mere boy. They refused to agree that Arthur should be King. From then until the next Christmas and then to the following Easter, the quarrels raged, but Arthur gathered clever and faithful men around him. With Merlin's guidance, he learned how to lead men and to win battles, and eventually he was crowned High King of England.

Sir Ector and Sir Kay stayed with Arthur for the rest of their lives and became Knights of the Round Table. Arthur ruled his kingdom from his castle at Camelot and sent out his knights to right wrongs and to fight on behalf of the weak and helpless. He was a great and good King. Some people say that he never died, but is sleeping in a cave in the Welsh mountains, waiting to lead his country once again.

9

The Green Children

This story is told by two English chroniclers of the Middle Ages: Ralph of Coggeshall and William of Newbridge. The events are supposed to have taken place in the twelfth century, some say in the reign of King Stephen (1135–54). This would have been some two generations after the Norman Conquest, when the people of England were speaking a mixture of Old English and Norman-French.

One bright sunny day some villagers from St Mary's Woolpit in Suffolk found two children wandering about crying near a wolf-pit. The children, a girl and a younger boy, were just like normal humans in shape, but their skin and hair were bright green. The children seemed to be dazzled by the sunlight and were very confused. They spoke in a strange language and did not appear to understand what the villagers said to them.

Not knowing what else to do, the people of St Mary's took the children to the house of Sir Richard de Calne at Wikes. His was the biggest household in the district and he had room to shelter the children. Even Sir Richard, who was a man of the world and had travelled widely, could not understand what the children were saying. They were treated kindly and given meat and bread to eat. The children appeared to be hungry, but they pushed the bread and meat aside and continued to cry.

Then, by chance, some green broad beans were brought in from the gardens. Eagerly the children snatched at them, but opened the stalks instead of the pods. When they found no beans inside, they started crying again. A member of the household showed the children how to open the pods and find the fat beans inside. At last the children ate something and became less distressed.

The children stayed with Sir Richard de Calne. At first they would eat only green food and the boy became depressed and weak. Sadly he died after a few months, but the girl learned to eat the same food as the rest of the household.

She lost the green tint to her skin and hair and took on the appearance of a normal human being. After a year or two, she learnt to speak the Anglo-Norman language of the people and at last she was able to tell her story.

The girl said that she had lived in a land where the light was always dim and shadowy, and where all the animals and the people were green, as she had been. She said that her home was called St Martin's Land and that, although the people were Christian, she thought they also worshipped St Martin. The sun never rose in St Martin's Land, but a bright country could be seen far away, across a wide river.

One day she and her brother were tending their flocks, when they came to the entrance of a large cave. They heard the sound of sweet bells and could not resist going into the cave to see what was making the beautiful music.

On and on and up and up they wandered, through twisting passages, until suddenly they came out into brilliant sunlight. They had never seen the sun, nor such bright daylight before. Their eyes hurt and their heads ached. They blundered about in confusion and could not find their way back to the cave from which they had come. After hours and hours of wandering, when they were hungry and exhausted, they were found by the villagers.

Sir Richard ordered a search to be made for the entrance to the cave, but it was never found. The girl remained in service in Sir Richard's household and when she was grown up, she married a man from Lenna.

10

The Fisherman and the Rich Moor

The great landmass of Spain stretches south from the rest of Europe to within sight of the northern coast of Africa. Much of Spanish history is concerned with conflicts between the Moors of Africa and the Kings and Queens of Spain.

Once, long ago, a kindly Spanish fisherman lived in a comfortable house on the shores of the blue Mediterranean Sea. He made good catches of fine fish and he took care of his money. However, the fisherman knew that not everyone was as fortunate and sensible as he was, so on every Christian feast day, he would go into the streets and look for a man who was poor. Then he would invite the man home to eat a good meal and to live for one day in warmth and comfort.

One Christmas Day the fisherman went out as usual in search of a poor man and he saw a Moorish slave who was thin and miserable-looking. At first the fisherman hesitated, because the Moors were Muslims and the Moorish pirates were always raiding the Mediterranean coast. They were hated and dreaded by the Spaniards. If a Moor was hungry and unhappy, then it was only what he deserved, they said.

But the fisherman thought to himself, 'It is Christmas. I must be generous to my enemy. It is easy to be kind to those who deserve kindness. Today I must help this poor man, even if he deserves to be a slave.'

The fisherman invited the Moor home with him, gave him warm clothes, sat him in a comfortable seat near the fire and fed him well. The Moor was surprised and grateful. At the end of the day he returned to his master.

Shortly afterwards the fisherman learned that the Moor had been ransomed by his family with a large sum of money and had returned to Africa. That seemed to be the end of the matter and the fisherman continued with his good works and his fishing.

A year or so later, while he was fishing far out at sea, the fisherman was captured by Moorish pirates and taken to the slave market in Algiers. He stood in chains, waiting to be sold and thinking of the miserable life that lay ahead of him. He scarcely bothered to look at the rich Moors who came to inspect him. One master would no doubt be as harsh as another. One Moor stopped and looked closely at the fisherman. He bought him at once and took him home.

Then he said, 'Aren't you the fisherman who takes poor unfortunate men into your home on feast days?'

'Yes, master,' replied the fisherman in surprise.

Then looking more closely at the Moor, he recognized him as the man he had entertained at his fireside one Christmas Day.

'I will repay one good deed with another,' smiled the Moor, and he freed the fisherman and arranged for him to be shipped home.

'But take my advice,' called the Moor, as the fisherman was leaving, 'you are growing old. Do not go to sea again. Stay by your fireside where pirates cannot capture you.'

The fisherman took that good advice and lived the rest of his life comfortably in his own home, thanks to the gratitude of the Moor.

11

The Pedlar of Swaffham

This story dates from the Middle Ages, when London Bridge was lined on both sides with shops and houses. The legendary pedlar is commemorated in Swaffham's town sign and there is a carved statue of him inside the church.

Legend has it that hundreds of years ago, in the village of Swaffham in the county of Norfolk in England, there lived a pedlar who was constantly having a certain dream. A voice told the pedlar that, if he went and stood on London Bridge, he would hear joyful news.

At first the pedlar took no notice. A journey to London would not be easy. It was nearly one hundred miles to London, so it would take him two or three days to walk there. And he would have to sleep in barns or hedges along the way.

But the dreams persisted, and the voice was so insistent that the pedlar became upset and worried. He began to dread going upstairs to bed.

At last he said to his wife, 'It is no use. I shall have to go to London and stand on London Bridge or I shall have no peace for the rest of my life.'

He packed a few belongings, some food and a little money. He whistled up his dog and they walked the long road to London.

In those days London Bridge was a bustling place with houses and shops on either side of the roadway. It was the only way across the Thames unless you went by boat. For several days the pedlar stood on the bridge, first in one spot and then another, but no one spoke to him and no one gave him joyful news.

I was a fool to come, he told himself, but still he waited.

Finally, when he had nothing but a crust of bread in his pocket and knew that he must leave for Norfolk within the hour, a shopkeeper stepped out of his shop and came and spoke to him.

'Satisfy my curiosity,' said the shopkeeper. 'I have seen you here for several days. You do not beg, you do not pick pockets, you are not selling anything. Why are you standing here?'

The pedlar replied honestly that he had dreamed that if he stood on London Bridge, he would hear joyful news.

The shopkeeper burst out laughing. 'You don't want to take any notice of foolish dreams,' he said. 'I keep having this dream that if I go to Swaffham in Norfolk – a place I know nothing of – and ask for the pedlar's house and go into the orchard at the back and dig under a great oak tree, then I will find a hoard of treasure. What nonsense! I am sure that if I took any notice of that dream, I would make a long journey to Swaffham and find nothing when I got there. You be off home, my friend, and take no notice of your dreams.'

The pedlar hurried home to Swaffham. He went into the orchard at the back of his house and dug under the great oak tree. He found a chest of treasure and was wealthy for the rest of his life.

12

The Lost Islands

Parts of the coastland in the west of Britain are sinking. In several places, at a particularly low tide, stumps of old forests and remains of ancient villages can be seen sticking up out of the sea. People say that if you sit on the seashore and listen, you can hear the old church bells tolling as they rock to and fro with the tide.

Hundreds of years ago the Little People, or Faery Folk, lived all over Britain. Now, after many invasions and with the noise of modern life, the Little People have retreated to live in the lonely places of Wales and Scotland and Cornwall. They are a secretive people and keep themselves to themselves, but some of the old Celtic folk, who have the power of second sight, can see them. The Little People dress in green, except for their hats, which are red. It does not do to offend them, for they have magical powers.

Most people think it is wise to stay right away from the Little People. However, one Welshman became rich from mixing with the faeries. His name was Griffith and he lived in a town on the Welsh coast called Milford Haven.

Many years ago, large markets were held at Milford Haven. The country people for miles around brought their goods to sell. The Little People came to the market too. They never spoke, but if they wanted to buy anything, they would put down money beside it. If the stallholder thought the price was fair, he would pick the money up. The faeries would then take the goods and go. If the price was not enough, the stallholder would leave the money lying until more was added to it, or until the faeries took up the money and left without buying anything.

The faeries who went to Milford Haven market were honest. They never stole and the local people were glad to trade with them. However, very few people could see the faeries; most traders merely saw the money appearing on their stalls and the goods being taken. One man, a corn merchant called Griffith, could always see the Little People and so could a butcher who lived in the centre of town. Griffith and the butcher sold a lot of corn and meat to their faery customers.

'There must be plenty of them to need all those supplies,' Griffith would say to the butcher.

'Indeed,' the butcher replied. 'And where do they live, I ask myself. It can't be in the valleys round here because I see no sign of them when I walk my dog. Either they must be too lazy to grow food for themselves, or they must live somewhere where there is no room to farm.'

Everyone wondered where the Faery Folk lived, but no one could find out. Then one day Griffith was walking high up by St David's churchyard when he happened to glance out to sea and saw some islands where he had never seen islands before. Griffith had inherited the second sight from his mother, and knew that these were the Green Isles of the Ocean, the islands that had been swallowed by the sea long ago.

'If the islands are in the mood to show themselves, then I will go out to look at them,' he thought.

He started to go down towards the seashore, but the islands disappeared immediately. But when he walked back up to St David's churchyard, he could see them again.

Griffith understood at once what was happening. 'I can only see the islands when I am standing on sacred land,' he muttered.

An ordinary man would have stayed in the churchyard and admired the islands from there, but Griffith was clever. He cut around the piece of turf on which he was standing and carried it down to his boat. Then he stood on the turf in the boat. When he looked seawards, he could see the islands clearly.

Standing on the turf all the way, Griffith sailed towards the islands and landed on the largest one. He was met by some of the Little People who had bought corn from him in Milford Haven. They greeted him with surprise and laughed when they heard how he had found his way to their home. Then they showed him the beauties of their little islands.

'Many of these islands have disappeared beneath the waves,' they said, 'but some have become invisible by magic and it is on these islands that we live, safe from you big, trampling mortals.'

They sent Griffith home with his arms full of gifts and they continued to trade with him for many years. He became a rich man. However, the faeries made Griffith give them the turf from the churchyard, and no matter how often he stood in St David's churchyard staring out to sea, he never saw the islands again.

13

The Lambton Worm

The worm is often referred to in old English stories. It was a monstrous, fearsome creature rather like a serpent. Story tellers obviously assumed that worms were well-known to their listeners. Whatever these terrible beasts were that crept over England eight hundred years ago, they are not seen nowadays. However, the River Wear and the town of Chester-le-Street still lie in the north of England, and the well is known as Worm Well.

Long ago, in the eleventh century, the son and heir of Lambton Castle in England respected neither God nor man. He did not perform his duties on his family estates, nor did he go to church. If anything displeased him, he cursed and swore in a loud voice, to the dismay of all who heard him.

One Sunday morning, after a night of drinking, the young man went fishing in the River Wear. He cast his line many times over the water, but he did not catch anything. People on their way to the chapel at Brugeford heard the Heir of Lambton cursing and swearing, and were very shocked.

Just as the church service was starting, there was a tug on the fishing line. Thinking that at last he had caught a fine fish, the young man hauled in his catch, only to find that it was a horrible serpent-like worm. Cursing his luck yet again, the Heir snatched the loathsome worm off his line and threw it into a nearby well.

Not many weeks after this incident, the Heir of Lambton went off to the Holy Land on a crusade. Some thought he had repented of his wicked ways. Others said it was because his family wanted to have a rest from him and hoped that the experience of a long voyage abroad would teach the young man some sense.

Meanwhile, the worm stayed in the well. It quickly became longer and larger until it outgrew the well and crawled down to the river. During the day it curled round a rock and at night it lay at the foot of a nearby hill. In a month or two it was long enough to wind itself round the hill three times. The local people called it Worm Hill from that time on.

At first the horrible worm was content to hunt in the wild, but as it grew larger, it began to prey on domestic animals. It drank

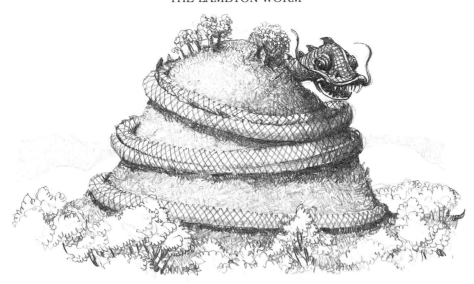

milk from the cows, ate chickens and lambs, and chased the dogs and the horses. As the months went by, it needed more and more food and soon the land to the north of the river was stripped bare. The farms were deserted because no one dared to live there.

Then the worm turned its eyes to the southern side of the river, where Lambton Castle stood. The land was rich and the animals well-fed and fat. The worm slithered across the river bed and wriggled towards the castle, leaving a loathsome slimy trail behind it. The Lord of Lambton was old now and his fighting days were over. No one knew what to do. Everyone panicked and wished that the Heir of Lambton had been a more dutiful son. He should have been with them now to defend the castle.

At last a steward spoke up and suggested that, as they were not fortunate enough to have a young fighting lord, they should try to placate the worm. Perhaps, in that way, they might be spared.

'I have heard,' said the steward, 'that the worm likes milk. Let's fill the trough in the courtyard with milk and hope that the worm will be satisfied.'

The loathsome worm slid into the courtyard, drank the milk and retired across the River Wear. It wound itself around its hill and went to sleep without doing any further harm.

The next day the worm approached Lambton Castle again. Again the trough was filled. It took the milk from nine cows to fill the trough and so the household had to do without. This caused discontent in the servants' hall because there was no pudding for supper. Why should the servants do without their pudding just because Lord Lambton was old, and his heir did not know his duty? Perhaps the trough could be only half filled?

The next day, when the worm again slithered towards Lambton Hall, the milk from five cows was put into the trough, and the milk from the other four cows was given to the servants. The worm flew into a rage and lashed furiously with its tail, uprooting valuable trees from the castle park.

'This is too bad,' old Lord Lambton roused himself to say. 'My great-grandfather planted those trees. I can't have them uprooted by a worm. The servants will have to do without the milk and that is that.'

The worm terrorised the whole neighbourhood. Knights and other brave men tried to slay the fearsome creature, but they all failed and died in the attempt. Though they fought bravely, the worm had the power to join itself back together wherever it had been cut in half. The worm resisted everyone who came to slay it and stayed in possession of Worm Hill.

After seven years, the Heir of Lambton returned from the Crusades. He was now reformed, and looked forward to taking his place in due courseas Lord of Lambton. But he found that things had changed while he was away. The property was now a wasteland, the servants were a terrified rabble, and his dear father was sinking white-haired into his grave.

'Really, this is too bad!' he sighed. 'Can't a fellow sow a few wild oats and turn his back for a year or two without the place going to pieces entirely? I knew I would have to fight the heathens and sort things out abroad, but I did expect everything to be all right here in England.'

The servants told the Heir how a huge worm was terrorising the whole neighbourhood and had killed every man who tried to slay it. He crossed over the river to see the worm, which lay curled round the root of Worm Hill, fast asleep. It was certainly a huge and loathsome monster.

Unsure what would be the best way of handling the situation the Heir went to consult the Wise Woman of Chester-le-Street. He had learned many useful things during the Crusades, and one of them was to think before acting.

He was not well received.

'All this trouble is your fault,' she screeched. 'If you had not pulled the worm from the river and thrown it into the well and cursed and blasphemed on the sabbath day, none of this would have happened. I don't know how you have the courage to show your face among respectable people!'

'Yes, yes, well I'm frightfully sorry, but we're all young once,'

said the Heir, 'and now I am here to put things right. Can you forget what happened in the past and give me some good advice?'

Seeing that the Heir was now a reformed man, the Wise Woman of Chester-le-Street decided to give him the benefit of her wisdom. 'Have your best suit of mail studded with spearheads, and hold your best sword in your hands,' she said. 'Then when you fight the worm, stand on a rock in the middle of the River Wear and confront it face to face. Put your trust in God. If you are fortunate enough to overcome the worm, you must slay the first living creature you meet on your way home. Otherwise, for nine generations, no Lord of Lambton will die in his bed.'

The Heir thanked the Wise Woman and returned to Lambton Castle. He sent his strongest suit of mail to be studded with spearheads. He prayed in Brugeford chapel and swore a solemn oath that he would fight the worm with all his strength and, if he overcame it, that he would slay the first living creature he met on his way home.

When his armour was ready, the Heir of Lambton took his finest sword in his hand and, at the hour when the worm usually awoke, took his stand on a rock in the middle of the River Wear. Soon the horrible monster uncoiled its slimy length from around Worm Hill and slithered towards the river. It swam southwards towards the lands of Lambton and as it passed the Heir, he struck it on the head.

Flying into a rage, the monster turned and swiftly coiled its tail round the Heir, planning to crush him to death as it had crushed so many others. However, the Wise Woman of Chester-le-Street had given good advice. As the worm pulled its coils tighter, it wounded itself on the spearheads that studded the Heir's armour. It howled with pain as gaping holes were torn in its flesh, and the river ran with blood.

Pulling his arms free from the thrashing coils, the Heir hacked at the worm with his sword. Again he was grateful for the Wise Woman's advice. As he slashed pieces from the worm's enormous coils, they were carried away down the river. Had they been fighting on land, the worm would have been able to join itself back together again. After a fierce and desperate struggle the worm was dead at last. The Heir of Lambton was exhausted, but alive and victorious.

During the fight the household at Lambton remained locked up inside the castle, praying for victory for their young lord. The Heir had told them that, when the worm was slain, he would blow a blast on his bugle. Then they were to release an old hound so that he might slay it as the first living thing to meet him after his victory.

The Heir, triumphant with success, blew a huge blast on his horn and started to walk back to Lambton Castle. He saw the gates open, but then his heart turned to ice. His beloved father ran out, laughing with joy that his brave son was safe. In his happiness, the old man had forgotten about his son's promise to kill the first living thing to meet him on the way home.

Filled with horror, the Heir blew another blast on his horn and the old hound came bounding from the gates. But it was too late. The father reached his son a stride before the hound came leaping up at him.

The Heir stared at his sword, still dripping with the worm's blood. 'Who but we three knows who reached me first?' he thought, as he plunged the blade into the hound.

So peace and prosperity returned to the lands of Lambton, and those around them. The Heir married the daughter of a neighbouring Lord and produced his own son and heir.

However, the Fates were not to be defied. The vow had been broken. For nine generations, the Lords of Lambton met violent deaths.

14

St Mark and the Saving of Venice

Venice is an ancient Italian merchant city. Built on low islands in a lagoon and scarcely above sea level, it is in constant danger from storms blowing in from the Adriatic Sea.

Once, long ago, an old fisherman lived in the city of Venice. He was a poor man without a home of his own, but he had fishing nets and his own boat. Each night he tied up in the shelter of a bridge near the Doge's palace to sleep. He was happy enough.

One February, there was a terrible storm. The wind howled and the sea rose higher and higher. The fisherman's boat was torn from its moorings and washed out towards the open sea. After a great struggle, the frightened man managed to land near St Mark's Cathedral. Wet and shivering, he waited for dawn. He prayed for the storm to abate, but it grew worse and the night became blacker. The fisherman feared that the end of the world had come.

Suddenly a stranger walked down the steps from St Mark's Cathedral. 'Will you row me across to the church of St George?' he asked, pointing across the Grand Canal to the island opposite.

'Are you mad?' gasped the fisherman. 'No ship could cross that raging sea, least of all my little boat.'

'We will come to no harm,' replied the man. 'And I will pay you well, for I must reach St George's church tonight.'

The fisherman shrugged. He liked the idea of earning good pay and the island was not far off – perhaps he could reach it safely. He set off with the stranger and, to his amazement, the waves became smooth in his path and he easily reached St George.

'Wait for me,' instructed the stranger, stepping ashore. In a few minutes he returned with a handsome young knight dressed in full armour. They stepped into the boat and asked the fisherman to row them to the church of St Nicolas di Lido.

'That is a long way away!' gasped the poor fisherman. 'If we try

to go there, we will all be drowned for certain sure.'

'I will pay you well,' said the stranger, 'and we will be safe.'

Something in the man's manner reassured the fisherman and again he launched his little boat into the huge waves and lashing wind. Again the sea turned calm in their path and they reached their destination safely. At St Nicolas di Lido the two passengers went ashore and came back with an old man dressed as a bishop.

'Have no fear,' he said, smiling at the fisherman. 'but row us three between the two castles that guard the way to the open sea.'

The fisherman was horrified, because this was the place where the sea raced and roared worst of all. But he felt that he could not refuse after going so far.

He rowed his little boat between the two castles and then he almost died of fright. Advancing between the castles, with all sails set, was a huge black ship filled with screaming demons. 'Venice!' they shrieked. 'Venice! We will have Venice tonight!'

The black ship surged onwards with the horrible demons leaning over the rails. They reached out their grasping, scaly hands towards the beautiful palaces of Venice, laughing to each other and shrieking in tune with the howling wind.

'Row us into the path of that ship!' ordered the young knight.

The fisherman obeyed. Then he saw the stranger from St Mark, and the young knight from St George, and the bishop from St Nicolas di Lido, stand up boldly. With no hint of fear, they made the sign of the cross at the ship of howling demons. At once it disappeared and the sea became calm.

The trembling fisherman rowed each man back to the place he had come from, but at St Mark's Cathedral he asked for the good pay that had been promised to him.

The first stranger took a gold ring from his finger. 'I am St Mark,' he said. 'Tonight you took me and St George and the bishop, St Nicolas, to save Venice from those demons. This is St Mark's ring from the city treasury. Show it to the Doge, the ruler of Venice; tell him your story and he will reward you.'

Next day the fisherman did as he was told. The Doge searched the treasury, but St Mark's ring was missing. Then the Doge believed the fisherman's story. He rewarded him and ordered a great procession of thanksgiving to go from St Mark's Cathedral to the island of St George and then out to St Nicolas di Lido.

Beneath the bridge where the fisherman used to shelter is carved a picture of the Madonna with a fishing boat, in memory of the brave old man.

15

The Legend of the Lorelei

The River Rhine is one of the great waterways of Europe. It flows through Switzerland, Germany and then across the lowlands of Holland into the North Sea. Mountains, forests and castles line its route, and dark, melancholy legends are told about those who lived on its banks.

Just north of the city of Koblenz in Germany, the Lorelei Rock juts out above the River Rhine. Nowadays tourists look up at the great rock in wonder, but in days gone by, people looked up at it with fear and kept off the river as daylight faded.

Many years ago, a beautiful but heartless water nymph lived at the top of the Lorelei. Her hair was golden, her skin was white, and her curved lips were pink. As a girl the nymph had drowned herself in the river Rhine because her lover was unfaithful.

Every evening the water nymph became visible to human eyes and no man could resist her beauty nor the loveliness of her song. Sailors foolish enough to be near the Lorelei at sunset would steer their boats straight for the huge rock. As they stared up at the lovely nymph, their craft would be dashed to pieces and the unfortunate men would drown in the cold waters of the river.

Ronald, the son of the Count Palatine, swore that he would outwit the Lorelei. 'I will not be drowned,' he boasted. 'I will climb the rock and seize the Lorelei maiden and make her my wife.'

He bribed a fisherman to row him towards the huge rock at sunset. Through the twilight they saw the white form of the nymph as she shook out her golden hair. Ronald heard her teasing voice singing and laughing.

'You are not rowing fast enough,' he shouted at the fisherman. 'She will vanish before I can climb the rock.'

But the fisherman was rowing slowly and cautiously. He did not want his boat dashed to pieces, as so many others had been.

'Faster!' shrieked Ronald, and when the fisherman would not obey him, the young man threw himself into the water, swam towards the rock and was swept away and drowned like all the other young men who had tried to capture the lovely Lorelei. The heartless nymph laughed until dawn hid her from human sight.

The Count Palatine was heartbroken. He gave orders that the nymph must be killed so that she could lure no more men to their deaths.

The next day four tough old soldiers made their way towards the high rock. They were skilled mountain climbers and easily scaled the rock. As evening fell and the Lorelei nymph appeared, it was clear that she would soon be within their reach.

'We will fling you from the top of the rock into the river below,' they shouted. 'You will be dashed to pieces and that will be the end of you and your evil ways.'

For a moment the nymph faltered and seemed afraid, then she gave a shaky laugh. 'The Rhine is my father,' she said. 'He will not let you harm me. He will save me from you.'

She took the pearls that were twisted in her hair and the necklaces from around her throat. Then she tore the strings of jewels apart and leaning far out over the river, she threw the precious stones one at a time into the rushing torrent.

'Father! Father!' she called. 'Save me! Waters of the Rhine, carry these stones to my father, tell him I am in danger. Ask him to send his foaming steeds to save me from my enemies.'

Then the waters of the Rhine seethed and roared and rose up like two white horses. They washed over the top of the rock, carrying the Lorelei maiden away and out of sight. Never again did she sing from the heights above the river.

The soldiers, who had clung on like limpets while the waters washed over the rock, hurried home and told the Count Palatine that the nymph was gone. Everyone rejoiced that no more men would be lured to their deaths. But the count mourned his dear son for the rest of his life.

16

The Smith and the Little People

The Celts lived in the British Isles before and during the Roman occupation. When the Roman legions finally withdrew in about 425 AD, there were fresh invasions by the Angles and Saxons, who conquered most of the area now known as England. The Celts were driven back to Wales, Scotland and Ireland, and the small islands along the west coast. The Celts have a great fund of stories about the Little People, or faeries, and their tricks.

Not so many years ago, on one of the islands washed by the cold green Atlantic Ocean, a blacksmith lived with his only son. The boy was strong and healthy, and the joy of his father's heart.

When the lad was fourteen years old, he fell ill and took to his bed, exhausted and depressed. No one could find what was wrong with him. Nothing could cure him. He just lay there – thin, pale and old-looking. People whispered that he would soon be dead.

Strange to say, the boy did not die. Month in, month out, he lay on the bed, but to the amazement of his father, he developed an enormous appetite. He ate everything that was set before him and then called for more. His distressed father was worn out and became poor because he had to buy so much food for his lazy shrivelled son.

One day a Wise Man happened to visit the forge where the blacksmith worked, and asked the smith why he looked so sad. When he heard the story, he said, 'I am sure it is no longer your son who lies on that bed. That is a changeling, a faery substitute. Your son has been stolen by the Little People.'

The smith became more distressed than ever. 'I thought so! I thought so!' he groaned. 'My poor dear son! What can I do to rescue him?'

'You must find the courage to stand against the Little People,' said the Wise Man. 'Can you do that?'

'To save my son, I can,' replied the smith.

'Then first we must make sure that I am right, and then we must get rid of the changeling,' said the Wise Man.

He told the smith to collect as many empty eggshells as he could from his friends. He was to take them into the boy's bedroom together with a bucket of water. Then he was to fill the eggshells with water and carry them, two at a time, across the room as if they were very heavy, and set them down with great effort at the side of the bed, in sight of his son.

The smith did as he was told, and as he set the eggshells down, a voice called from his son's throat, 'Ah ha! How stupid! I have lived for five hundred years and I have never before seen anyone foolish enough to try and carry water in eggshells.'

The smith was now certain that his son was gone and that a changeling lay in his bed. He again consulted the Wise Man.

'I have serious news for you,' sighed the Wise Man. 'If the changeling is one of the Little People, then they have taken your son into the Green Knole.'

He pointed to the huge green hill that had stood outside the village since before time began.

The poor smith went pale. 'How will we ever get my son free from that place?' he asked.

'Have courage and do exactly as I say,' replied the Wise Man.

This time he told the smith to light a huge fire at the side of the changeling's bed, and when the creature asked what the fire was for, to say that he would see presently. Then, when the fire was roaring and red, the smith was to pick up the changeling and fling him into the hottest part.

'If we have been mistaken and the invalid really is your son, he will beg you to save him and you must pull him back,' said the Wise Man. 'But if he is the changeling, then he will say nothing but fly away through the roof.'

The smith returned home and built a huge fire at the side of his son's bed.

The thin creature on the bed stared at the flames with fear in his eyes. 'Why are you building that fire?' he asked.

'I will show you presently,' replied the smith. And when the fire was blazing red, he picked up the lad and tried to toss him on the flames. A weird cry rang through the house. A terrible flapping noise filled the room, then there was a crash as a hole appeared in the roof, and the boy was gone.

'That is good news indeed. Everything is going well,' smiled the Wise Man, when the poor exhausted smith told him what had happened. 'Now you will really need all your courage to snatch your son back from inside the Green Knole.'

He told the smith that once a month, on the night of the full moon, a door opened in the side of the Green Knole.

'You must take a Bible to defend yourself against the anger of the Little People, a sword with which to block open the door, and a crowing cock hidden under your coat. You must go through that door and enter the Green Knole,' said the Wise Man. 'You will find yourself in a fine large room full of Little People. Working at a forge at the far end you will see your son. You must take him by the arm and pull him out of the Green Knole with you. The Little People will try to stop you, but if you are firm, you will succeed.'

At the next full moon, the unhappy smith stood before the Green Knole. His heart was thundering in his breast and he almost fainted with fear as he saw a door swing open in the grassy side of the hill. Jamming the door open with his sword, the smith walked forward and found himself in dazzling light. The room was filled with Little People laughing and chattering. At the far end he could see his son, stooped and tired from working as a slave all those long months.

As the smith pushed his way through the laughing, dancing Little People, who turned and frowned at him.

'What do you want here?' shouted one.

'I have come for my son. He must stay here no longer,' replied the smith.

The Little People shouted with rage and snatched at the smith's arms. He clasped the Bible firmly and no harm came to him. More Little People crowded round, jostling the smith and trying to push him from the Knole. This time the cock struggled out from under the smith's coat. It crowed and flapped round the room.

The Little People were startled. They wondered if dawn had come and daylight was about to burst into the room. In the confusion that followed the smith caught his son's arm and dragged him to the doorway. Then they found themselves rolling out into the fresh air. The sword was thrown after them and the door slammed shut.

The smith took his son home. It was indeed his own son, with all his sweet loving ways, but he was not as he used to be. He sat quietly in a corner and would not speak at all. 'The Little Folk might just as well have kept him,' sighed his heartbroken father.

A year and a day after the escape from the Green Knole, the smith was making a sword for an important gentleman who had ordered the finest work that the smith could do. Try as he might, the smith could not get the blade the way he wanted it.

Suddenly, to his surprise, his son came to stand at his side. 'Give the sword to me,' he said. Taking the metal, he worked it in the most delicate way until he had made the finest weapon that the smith had ever seen.

After that the enchantment seemed to drop away from the boy. He became a normal cheerful lad and grew into a fine young man. He was never bothered again by the Little People from the Green Knole. He had, however, learned something in his months with the Little People, for he became the finest swordmaker in all the islands and he and his father became rich men.

17

The Grey Palfrey

Towards the end of the Middle Ages, life in Europe became a little less grim. The scourge of the Black Death had come and gone. Large national groupings were emerging to form the countries we know today. Feuds and fighting between local barons suddenly seemed old-fashioned. At last there was time to think of more than basic survival. Young people began to feel there should be more to marriage than property contracts. There was talk of love and happiness. In France minstrels told the romantic tales that were the forerunners of our modern novels.

Long ago, a handsome young knight called Guy lived in the Champagne region of France. He was brave and strong, but he was not wealthy. All he owned was a small manor house and a few fields deep in a forest away from the highways.

Poor though he was, Guy had one possession that was the envy of everyone in the neighbourhood. He owned a splendid grey palfrey. This pretty riding horse had the finest limbs, and was the best-trained animal ever seen in the kingdom. Many noblemen who were richer than the young knight offered to buy the grey palfrey, but he would not part with it.

'I trained it and it is mine to serve me and to be my friend,' he said, with more truth than he realised.

Being of noble birth, Guy was invited to the social gatherings at the great aristocratic houses of Champagne. Everyone knew and liked him, but as he was blessed with few of this world's goods, he was not considered important. At dinner he was seated far away from the grand people at the head of the table. No mother put him on the list of desirable husbands for her daughter. However, the brave young knight's handsome face caught the eye of a great duke's daughter. She fell in love with him and he with her. They met in secret, but they knew their love was hopeless.

The Duke's daughter, who was called Isabel, knew that her father would arrange for her to marry a wealthy man. The brave knight knew that without a rich property he could never ask a duke for his daughter's hand in marriage.

Fortunately for the young couple, the Duke's home was in the forest not far from Guy's manor house. Whenever he could, the knight rode through the narrow forest paths to the walls of the Duke's great house. At a little barred grating hidden among the bushes he would wait for his beloved.

Isabel slipped away to talk to her knight whenever she could. She touched his hand through the opening in the wall and whispered words of love. Then Guy rode home singing with happiness. But if he waited at the wall in vain while she stayed in the house, unable to slip away to join him, then he rode back through the forest filled with misery. Tears ran down his cheeks as he slumped in the saddle of the grey palfrey, scarcely noticing where he went.

Several years passed in this way, for Guy and Isabel were both young. The knight was brave and fearless, and as he grew to the full strength of his manhood, he achieved more and more success at the great tournaments.

In those days all young men of noble blood learned to be skilled fighters. Mock battles called tournaments were regularly held, and the winners took the armour and horses of their opponents. These trophies were often of considerable value and after several victories, Guy was able to put some coffers of gold in his strong room. The knight began to wonder if, after all, he might dare to ask the Duke for the hand of his daughter.

I am not rich, but now I am not poor. My estate is small, but they support me, my family is noble and I am a skilled soldier. Surely the duke could welcome me as a son-in-law, he thought.

Wearing his finest clothes, he rode the grey palfrey to the Duke's castle and asked to speak to the great man. The Duke agreed to see him, for he had known Guy since boyhood.

Guy bowed. 'Your Grace,' he said, 'you see before you a skilled soldier and an honest man able to manage men and estates. You see a man fit to be a member of your household. I have a request to ask of you.'

The duke looked at the knight in astonishment. 'Surely you are not asking for employment,' he said. 'Nobles do not work. They fight and live off their estates. You know that.'

Guy smiled. 'Indeed I do. I am not seeking employment, I am trying to persuade you that I am fit to marry your daughter. We have loved each other for a long time. Our feelings will never change. Will you give me your daughter's hand in marriage?'

The Duke laughed until the tears ran down his cheeks. 'Have you gone mad?' he asked. 'My daughter is my only child and will inherit my vast property. She must marry a man equally rich. I will not waste her on a boy with a few bags of gold in his shabby manor house.'

Then the Duke smiled at the young man in a kindly way, for he had known him since he was a child. 'Go home and forget such foolish dreams,' he said. 'Busy yourself at your tournaments. One day you will find the daughter of another poor nobleman, living in a manor house like yours, and she will suit you very well.'

Guy turned away with a heavy heart. He rode his grey palfrey home through the secret paths of the forest. The next day he set off for a tournament in southern France. 'If I win enough, then one day perhaps the Duke might relent,' he thought.

The young knight was away from Champagne for many weeks, and during that time an old friend of the Duke's came visiting. This man was as old and grey-haired as the Duke himself, and both were miserly by nature. The friend looked with envy at the Duke's fine home and rich lands, for although he had much property, he still wanted more. The old comrades sat talking of days gone by and of long-dead men and women whose faces would never smile at them again.

'Ah, how I miss my wife,' sighed the friend. 'Being left a widower is a lonely fate.'

Then the Duke looked at his friend and said, 'I am a wealthy man and you are a wealthy man. Joined together we would be richer than anyone else in France. If you were to marry my daughter, we could manage our affairs to our mutual benefit. No one would be more powerful than we two combined.'

His friend liked the Duke's idea. 'With such an arrangement, I would marry your daughter without asking for a dowry,' he said. 'The income of our joint properties would bring profit enough.'

When he heard those words, the Duke had no more doubts. 'Let us make arrangements for the marriage to take place as soon as possible,' he said.

When the Duke's young daughter heard that she was to marry her father's grey-haired old friend, she was heartbroken. She begged the Duke not to make her do such a thing.

'If I may not marry my beloved knight who lives in his manor house in the forest, at least let me wed a young man,' she pleaded. 'Do not tie me to a wrinkled old miser.'

The Duke brushed her pleas aside. 'I brought you up so that you could make a marriage to improve our family fortunes,' he said. 'This is the richest offer we will ever have. Do your duty and behave as a noblewoman should. Do not burden my ears with talk of happiness.'

The young woman returned to her room. She prepared a beautiful dress for her wedding day and she wept.

The Duke sent out invitations to his closest friends to be guests at the wedding. He summoned his steward and gave orders for food and for the preparation of chambers. Then he turned to his master of the horses.

'My daughter should ride to her wedding on a quiet, well-behaved mount,' he said, 'one with a fine appearance that will be the envy of everyone who sees her.'

'In that case,' replied the master of the horse, 'there is only one horse for her to ride. That is the grey palfrey belonging to the young knight who lives in the forest.'

'Of course,' smiled the Duke, 'that grey palfrey is the very mount we need. Send to Guy and ask him to lend me the horse on the day before the wedding. I will return it to him, well cared for, on the day after the ceremony.'

The Duke did not spare a thought for the feelings of the young knight. Great noblemen expected lesser nobles to oblige them with services and goods. That was the way of the world.

The Duke's servant arrived at the young knight's manor house just as he was returning triumphant from a great tournament. The servant asked if the Duke could borrow the palfrey for three days during the coming week.

'Of course,' replied Guy. 'It will be rested by then.' He was glad to do a favour to ingratiate himself with the father of his beloved. From idle curiosity he added, 'Why does the Duke need my horse next week? Is he going on a journey?'

'No,' said the servant. 'The horse is needed for the wedding of the duke's daughter. She will ride the grey palfrey to the church, where she will marry the duke's old friend. Everything is arranged for the two great estates to be joined together.'

The young man stood still and his heart turned cold. His beloved was to marry someone else. He would never know another happy hour. For a few moments he considered refusing to lend the grey palfrey. Why should he do anything to help this unwelcome marriage?

Then he thought, my beloved cannot wish to marry this old man. If I send her my horse, perhaps that will be a little comfort to her. In her unhappiness, she will have something of mine to remind her that we are at least united in our sorrow.

The next week Guy sent his horse to the Duke's home on the day before the wedding. Then he shut himself in his bedchamber and would speak to no one. He sat staring out of the window.

Meanwhile, the wedding guests had arrived at the Duke's home. The evening before the ceremony they all dined merrily together. They laughed and toasted the bridegroom and the Duke and congratulated them on their splendid alliance. They sat up

late, drinking the free wine, and stumbled to their beds scarcely an hour before they were due to rise.

Isabel also spent a sleepless night, but she did not pass her hours in jollity. Like Guy she sat staring from the window of her bedchamber. She thought of her grey-haired old bridegroom with his wrinkled skin and her own face set into lines of unhappiness.

The next morning, before dawn, the steward went round the house, hammering on the doors and calling to the guests to wake up and mount their horses. 'It is a long ride to the church,' he called, 'we must start at once.'

Groaning and clutching their aching heads, the Duke and the bridegroom and their friends staggered from their beds. In the half-light they dragged on their rich clothes and groped their way into their saddles. Two by two they jangled along the narrow forest road, keeping their heads down to avoid the sweeping branches of the overhanging trees. The Duke and the bridegroom rode at the head of the procession, and the Duke's daughter at the rear in the care of the steward. Isabel wore her lovely dress, but her eyes were blinded with tears. The steward, who had been up all night, dozed in his saddle.

So this bleary-eyed, belching company swayed through the forest in the dim grey light that shines before dawn. No one noticed when, from force of habit, the grey palfrey turned down the side path that was usually taken by Guy. Isabel sat in the saddle, cold and exhausted, and did not raise her head to look about her. Suddenly she wondered why the rest of the company had fallen so silent, then she saw that she was alone in the wilds of the forest on a narrow path in the middle of the forest. Terrified, she opened her mouth to call to the steward.

Then she closed her mouth and thought, 'I would rather be killed by wild beasts than go to the church to marry that old man. Let the grey palfrey carry me where it will.'

Back on the main track through the forest, the steward opened his eyes to see that the Duke's daughter no longer rode at his side. He thought she had gone ahead to be with her father, and with a grunt he went back to his snoozing.

The sun came up over the horizon. It cleared the tops of the trees and shone through the leaves. The grey palfrey tossed its head and hurried along the paths it had trod so many times.

Scenting home, the palfrey cantered across the last few yards of cleared land and pulled up snorting at the entrance to the young knight's manor house. The watchman pushed open a little grill high in the wall and looked out. 'Who is there?' he called.

Isabel was fearful that she had come to a den of bandits. However, she had little choice but to reply. 'I am lost in the forest. Please let me rest for a while and then show me the way to my home,' she called.

By this time the watchman had recognised the grey palfrey. He ran to his master's room and hammered on the door. 'Your grey palfrey is at the gate with a maiden as beautiful as the sun riding on its back,' he shouted.

Guy ran to the gates and flung them open. He saw the girl he loved sitting on his grey palfrey. She stared at him in astonishment. He led her in through the gates, and they were slammed shut after her.

Isabel slid from the horse into the arms of the brave young knight. 'How did you get here?' he asked.

'I don't know. I don't know!' She was sobbing and laughing at the same time. 'My eyes were blinded by tears. Somehow the grey palfrey turned away from the track and from the wedding guests and brought me here.'

'Then here you shall stay,' said the brave young knight. 'Our love was meant to be.' He woke the priest and called all his household together. With the whole household as witnesses, Guy and Isabel were married.

When the Duke and the bridegroom arrived at the church, they turned to wait for the Duke's daughter, while the whole company of groaning, sleepy guests dismounted from their horses. The steward arrived, but there was no bride.

Instantly there was uproar. Everyone dismounted and started shouting recriminations at each other. Then they mounted again and searched back through the forest and all over the Duke's large home. By the time they came to the young knight's manor house, the wedding was over. The couple were already man and wife, and what was done could not be undone.

The duke stamped with rage. Then, seeing there was nothing he could do, he gave the couple his blessing and left. Guy and Isabel lived the rest of their lives in happiness together.